EDUCATION OF TRIBAL WOMEN

EDUCATION OF TRIBAL WOMEN

A Comparative Study

By

P. Adinarayana Reddy

ANMOL PUBLICATIONS PVT. LTD.

NEW DELHI - 110 002 (INDIA)

ANMOL PUBLICATIONS PVT. LTD.
4374/4B, Ansari Road, Daryaganj
New Delhi - 110 002
Ph.: 23261597, 23278000
Visit us at: www.anmolpublications.com

Education of Tribal Women

First Published, 2004
ISBN 81-261-1831-8

PRINTED IN INDIA

Published by J.L. Kumar for Anmol Publications Pvt. Ltd., New Delhi - 110 002 and Printed at Mehra Offset Press, Delhi.

CONTENTS

ACKNOWLEDGEMENTS

Many people and institutions have helped me carrying out this work successfully. First and foremost my thanks goes to the Ministry of Tribal Affairs, Government of India for extending financial assistance for undertaking this work. I am also thankful to the officials of the ITDAs of Kerala and Andhra Pradesh for helping me in collecting the data from the remote tribal habitations.

I greatly appreciate and extend my thanks to Professor Dr. G. Prakash Reddy and Dr. T.V. Padmavathi, Institute for Development Research and Alternatives, Tirupati, for going through the manuscript and for suggestions.

I am also thankful to the Department of Adult Education, S.V. University, Tirupati for providing me all the facilities to carry out the project successfully. Further, the investigator also acknowledges the contribution and co-operation extended by Dr. D. Uma Devi, Dr. M. Obulesu, P. Viswanadha Gupta, Dr. Reddy Basha, Sri G. Eswaraiah, Sri B. Sudharshan Raju, Sri G. Surendra, Smt. R. Sampoorna and Sri K. Gnana Sekhar Reddy, Research Scholars, Department of Adult Education in the collection of the data and in analyzing the data. Not withstanding the help rendered by all the institutions and individuals the views expressed in this report are solely mine.

P. Adinarayana Reddy

CHAPTER - I

INTRODUCTION

India is the seventh largest country in the world in terms of area and second in terms of population. It is multicultural and multiracial with a tribal population of 6.77 crores (about 8 per cent of the total population of the country). It is estimated that the total number of tribal communities in India are about 461 (Singh,1966). The main characteristic features of Indian Tribes are variation in size of the population, inhabit all climatic zones, belong to all the four races— Negrito, Proto-Austroloid, Mongoloid and Caucasoid and use Indo-Aryan, Dravidian and Tibeto-Burman languages. All the groups are endogamous; monogamy is the predominant from of marriage but practice sororal polygamy and non-sororal polygamy. With the exception of politics and social affairs, women participate in almost all economic activities, rites and rituals. Tribesmen are not only peasants but also craftsmen and labourers. They do not suffer from any social stigma unlike the untouchable castes. A new educated and entrepreneurial elite class has emerged among them and this class is availing all the Governmental programmes including medical and health facilities. Unfortunately despite the existence of various kinds of policies, plans and programmes, tribals are still in the lowest economic strata of the society. They are being subjected for generations to various types of exploitation and discrimination.

Even today the widely pervasive reality in respect of tribal communities in India is that most of them are geographically isolated, economically weak, socially backward, but culturally rich and behaviourally simple and trustworthy, leading their life in the lap of nature. But they are facing a multiplicity of problems and difficulties which force them to lead a life at subsistence level and in a few cases full of poverty, deprivation, disadvantages and even various kinds of miseries and sorrows, very difficult to be effectively tackled by their own efforts and making it obligatory for the government in particular and society in general to intervene in a planned and organized manner.

Areas inhabited by tribes constitute a significant part of the regions of the country. On the whole, it is estimated that the predominant tribal areas comprise about 15 per cent of the total geographical area of the country. Their main concentrations are the central tribal belt in middle India and in the North east. About 50 per cent of the tribal population of the country is concentrated in the states of Chattisgarh, Jharkhand and Orissa. Besides, there is a sizeable tribal population in Maharashtra, Gujarat, Rajasthan, West Bengal, Andhra Pradesh, Tamilnadu and Kerala. The tribals in India live in forests, hills and naturally isolated regions. The isolated nature of the tribal regions and widespread poverty are acting against their integration in to the mainstream. The problem is that without destroying their culture, they have to be integrated with the mainstream as well as motivate them to march towards development. The tribes continue to remain economically and educationally backward and are languishing at the bottom of economic ladder. For generations together they are residing in inaccessible forest and hilly areas. They prefer to live in total isolation of the public and are fully secluded from the mainstream population. Their geographical isolation and impoverished economy have made them objects of economic exploitation. Except the traders and immigrants to tribal areas the general population in the country has very little knowledge about the tribes and the tribal areas. The traders and the immigrants use their knowledge to exploit the tribal communities.

The Constitution of India provides a comprehensive framework for the socio-economic development of tribes and for safeguarding them from exploitation from outside. Article 46 of the Constitution directs the State (both Central and State Governments) to promote with special care for the educational and economical interest of the weaker sections and specially tribes and to protect them from social injustice and all forms of exploitation. Keeping in view of the present situation of the tribal communities, the Government of India and respective State Governments initiated a number of development programmes for the socio-economic upliftment of the tribal communities. Among the various developmental programmes and schemes, education is given high priority.

Due to lack of education, the tribes lag behind in acquiring new skills required for the use of appropriate technology and other opportunities and have therefore failed to avail the benefits from the technological revolution that has greatly changed the economic scenario of the Indian society.

Moreover, education is the basic input for the development of human beings. Without proper educational inputs, it is beyond imagination to develop the Scheduled Tribes. Through education alone development issues relating to economic, cultural, health, nutrition etc., can be effectively communicated and managed. The basic impact of education on tribals particularly on women will be the increase in the standard of living of families, reduction in fertility rate and improvement of health and nutritional status. Female literacy has an important bearing on socio-economic conditions of the society. Unless women are educated, there is little scope for the socio-economic transformation. Further, education is considered as an instrument of social change. Investment has been made to strengthen the educational programmes and thus make it accessible to the deprived sections of the Indian society, more particularly to the ST and SC. Elaborate programmes of scholarship, reservation of seats in schools and colleges along with various other ancillary facilities are in operation. The Central and State Governments have provided the students belonging to the ST with many incentives, including freeship, scholarship, reservation of seats in educational institutions and Government Departments and establishment of separate hostels, ashram schools etc. It can be easily inferred that adequate spread of literacy among the ST is likely to enable them to compete with the upper classes on equal footing in the long run. Provision of educational facilities within the habitations is considered as an important factor positively contributing to the increase in the level of education among the tribes.

In spite of all the efforts of the Government, the formal system of education has failed to attract and retain the tribals into its fold resulting in large chunk of the tribes still lagging behind in terms of education when compared with general population. As a result, the policy makers and planners started searching for an alternative system to overcome the present situation. Recognising that literacy is the instant solution for bringing out immediate change in the life styles of the tribals, high priority was accorded in the National Adult Education Programme, New Policy on Education, 1986 and National Literacy Mission. In spite of all these efforts, the literacy rate among the tribals is very low and among the primitive tribal women in particular.

The position of literacy among tribes is extremely poor and poorest among the tribal women. Majority of the tribal women are illiterate. It would be an herculean task to bring about any social and economic change among the tribals if their literacy level does not improve in general and that of their women in particular.

In view of the above, an attempt is made to review the studies already conducted in the area of literacy of tribes. The available studies are categorized into three groups viz., studies related to tribal education, studies related to non-formal education in general and in particular among the tribal population and studies on adult education related to tribes. The available studies are as follows.

(a) Studies Related to Tribal Education

Several commissions and committees like Renuka Ray Committee (1959), Elwin Committee (1960) and Dhebar Commission (1962) suggested that opening of the Ashram Schools as an improvement over the existing pattern of education in scheduled areas.

Bose, A.B. (1970) states that the states with higher literacy in general population also have higher literacy in tribal population. He suggested that there were variations in the literacy levels among different tribes in a region.

Sachchidananda (1962) identified the irregularity in attendance and extent of dropout were much lower in the case of better accelerated tribes.

Verrier Elwin Committee (1960) states that a great deal of education was necessary for starting compulsory education for the tribes. Sachchidanada (1967), Ambasht (1970), Dasgupta (1963) and several others pointed out that retardation in education among tribal communities is due to apathy and indifferent attitude and lack of motivation for education which arises due to two main reasons, viz., Firstly, the formal education system is alien and not adjusted to their socio-economic and cultural needs. Secondly, the tribals have certain prejudices and suspicious towards sincerity of non-tribals.

Reddy, G.P. (1970) has found that the causes for wastage in tribal education in Andhra Pradesh, are due to poor economic conditions of the tribals and indifference of tribal parents towards education. Srivastava, L.R.N. (1970-71) and Sachchidananda (1967) have done a considerable work in this direction.

In a survey conducted by Tribal Cultural Research and Training Institute, Hyderabad (1971) revealed that there is rampant absenteeism, stagnation, and dropouts among the Chenchu schools in Andhra Pradesh. These triple evils are largely due to their ultimate constraints, poor economic conditions ingrained apathy towards education and lack of proper incentives to Chenchu students to make education attractive.

The Backward Classes Commission (Govt. of India, 1956), the Scheduled Areas and the Scheduled Tribes Commission (Govt. of India, 1962), Srivastava, L.R.N (1962) and others have pointed out that the slow progress of education among the tribals in India is due to inadequate provision of schools for these communities. The tribals generally live in inaccessible areas in small and scattered villages and therefore, schools are not available for all of them. Almost all the studies on tribal education in India pointed out that 'poverty' and 'neglect' happened to be the root cause for the slow progress of their education (Renuka Ray Committee, Govt. of India, 1959).

Khurana, G.K. (1978) in his article entitled, 'Approach to Education of Scheduled Tribes' pointed out that in spite of all the efforts to reduce the illiteracy among the Scheduled Tribes, the gap exists because of their poverty and backwardness coupled with ignorance and lack of educational facilities. He argued the need based education for adult tribals and alternative education methods for school age children.

Ratnayya (1978) in his study on structural constraints in tribal education in Andhra Pradesh, found that geographical barriers and inadequate school and hostel facilities in tribal areas. The salaried tribals sent their children to school more than the tribal farmers or labourers. The rate of dropout was tremendous from the 100 enrolled in the first standard only three persisted upto the fifth standard. The teachers from the tribal community were not adequately equipped with the languages of instruction. The non-tribal teachers had no orientation in tribal language and culture and as a result they were handicapped in achieving their objectives. The instructional material and the curricula were of the normal type and not specifically developed for the tribal children and hence they served the purpose inadequately.

Rebellow, M. (1978) found that curriculum is the main reason for high dropout rate in tribal areas at the primary stage. She suggested that the curricula should be need based keeping the local situations.

Sujatha, K. (1980) in her study concluded that household work and agricultural work and lack of interest on the part of Yanadi (Tribal) children for education were the main reason for poor enrolment in schools. There was a sharp fall in attendance during agricultural and rainy seasons. Free nature of Yanadi children and instability of family life due to frequent changes spouses did not help better enrolment. The curriculum was not related to the life and need of the Yanadi Community, so they found schooling meaningless, suffocating and realistic.

Kumar, R.Y. (1981) has studied the cause for non-enrolment, absenteeism and wastage. He has also analysed the impact of school system on the students and parents.

Dutta's (1983) study revealed that teaching and learning strategies need to be different for tribals.

Joshi (1985) in his study found that the majority of the tribes were very backward in their socio-economic and educational conditions. They were not fully conscious of their backwardness, exploitation and educational needs. Lack of accommodation and traveling facilities, location of schools, inconvenient school timings, shortage of materials were the major difficulties faced by the teachers in tribal areas.

Lakshmaiah and Yadappanaver (1986) observed that the schools, hostels and Ashram Schools were neither properly equipped and maintained nor the available institutions are adwquate to meet the requirement.

Lakshmaiah (1987) in his study identified the medium of instruction, and lack of sufficient finance, mis-utilization of stipend and scholarship, improper implementation of incentives and conflicting relations between the government and to her agencies as the problems in tribal schools in Bihar.

·Mahapatra, P.L. (1987) found that a low payment of monthly remuneration to the instructors was very discouraging location of the centres at a long distance away from their homes was causing distrurbance in the working conditions of women facilitators. The centres had poor physical facilities in terms of building, light arrangements, furniture, storage and display materials.

Shyamlal (1987) found that the unfavourable geographical conditions and low socio-economic level of the families act as constraints and as such there is more educational wastage among those living in the interior areas. The single teacher school seems to be the most important cause for dropout in the tribal area. At another level, the constraints for the spread of education among the tribals arises from low level of motivation and aspirations. He suggested that it is better to run the schools in the tribal areas during summer and other nonagricultural seasons and close them in the sowing and harvesting seasons because the tribal children help their parents in these seasons.

Sujatha (1987), reported that the Scheduled Tribes were out of formal education for centuries owing to structural constraints. Their geographical and social isolation kept them totally a loof from the development process.

Almelu (1990) conducted a study on problems of tribal education. She found that tribals were not willing to send their grown-up children to school because the worked as labour in supplementing family income. There is a long distance between the home and the school as they live in the mid forest and other remote areas. It is difficult to walk such long distance. Majority of the tribal areas does not have any transport facility and very few schools if there are schools, language is a big problem.

Ananthi Jebasingh (1990) showed that low socio-economic conditions of tribals centralized curriculum neither relateitself to the tribal situation nor appeal to their interests and the dual administration in the tribal schools also contribute their poor performance.

Dani (1991) found a number of impediments in the educational development of Buska tribe:

1. The first and foremost is the factor of their extreme poverty Owing to poverty the tribals do not send their children in houshold work or to earn a wage in minor agricultural work and both

2. Social and geographical isolation of the tribal communities in the cordial factor responsible for the slow progress of education among them.

3. The lack of edcuational institutions in Buska areas also is a barrier in their educational development.

4. The lack of positive attitude towards education among Buska is also a great barrier in their educational development.

Kulkarni (1991) in his study concluded that there is a physical distance between the school and the student. In hilly and forest tracts where steams flow, even this distance is too far. The parents are not willing to send their children to schools due to poverty and financial inability to afford to education, parents owing to lack of interest in education, want their children to help them at home. The present day practice is to teach the tribal students in the medium of the state language instead of their mother tongue. Shortage of teachers and the inadequacy of proper infrastructure are the other problems identified.

Patel (1991) in his study tribal education in India, a case study of Orissa found that wastage and stagnation are the greatest problems of education, particularly the school education in tribal areas and utilization of the educational facilities have not kept pace with the rapid expansion of the educational system, tending with lopsidedness, ill balanced development on the tribal educational front. Later the suggested that education among the tribals should focus on:

(a) Non-formal and adult education should be planned as complementary to formal education.

(b)The school timings as also vacations, should be fixed in tribal areas with reference to the local conditions which may be at variance with the timings and vacations in the state in region.

(c) Certain innovative institutional forms may be adopted in the special areas like sub-schools, pre-primary cum-primary institutions, elementary school complexes and residental schools in the seprately populated areas.

Subramanyam (1993) conducted a study on Gonds of Adilabad

District in Andhra Pradesh. He found that the Gonds and their children were faced with the problem of language. Owing to economic and social backwardness, the peoples participation in the educational programme is far from satisfactory.

(b) Studies related to Non-formal Education for General and Tribal Population

Rahman (1978) found that the curriculum materials (consisting of instructional material, teaching aid, instructional notes, instructor's manual) helped and in bringing about change of attitude among the learners towards matters pertaining to population.

Shah, A.J. (1979) stated that, the impact of NFE in the area of family planning was considerable. Regarding practices the impact on personal health was average where as an community health it was low. The impact of NFE in the use of user-time activity supplementary income area was high.

Karunakaran K. (1980) studied the factors that affected non-formal education and training of farmers were: availing of agricultural loans, prayers belief-is auspicious, in-auspicious are of fertilizers, high yielding variety of seeds, modern agricultural implements pesticides and reading habits. As the level of the education of the farmers increased by the influence of superstitious beliefs and customs decreased.

Sharma, M.L. (1980) revealed that in most cases the dropouts from primary schools, young women and those from lower socio-economic level were not provided any education; the adult were attracted only to the programmes concerned with literacy and numeracy. The facilitators the student, desired the use of audio-visual material. Shortage of funds prevented the implementation of skill development programmes. A majority of the students were satisfied with the physical facilities but not with the books and kids.

Dave, V.G. (1981) recommended that there should be one supervisor for every 30 centres and a good system of the training of

Instructor.The curriculum should have more content by local environment and rural based industries.The need for providing materials in timely and proper system of budget provision was emphasized to increase the enrolment of given area especially from tribal area, incentives should be provided.

Mullick, S.P. (1981) reviewed that the teacher trainees felt that tape-sliced materials were useful for non-formal education, making the lesson interesting and more useful in large classes. It was believed that it reduced the teacher's work load and was better than lecturer method.

Gupta, Daljit (1983) opined that attendance of children at the centres was found to be satisfactory.

Prabhakar Reddy (1983) studied non-formal educational needs of the rural community. He found that; (1) caste was perceived as main source of social evils; (2) rural community felt that education is must for a better livelihood, (3) tribal generally felt that they are not properly educated about development programmes, which are meant for them and (4) tribals felt that they have no access to formal education due to economic reasons.

Aolka, G.S. (1984) found that (1) the majority of the villagers were indifferent towards non-formal education programme due to lack of awareness and interest in the programmes, (2) if the non-formal education programmes were tied with vocational skill training environmental studies etc., these centres would attract more participants, (3) community needs were not property reflected in the curriculum, (4) instructors were not provided guides and manuals, (5) instructors of the opinion that the instructional material did not provide adequate illustrations and visual elements.

Kanta and Dutt (1984) found that some of the problems faced by the programme were low remunerative, for instructors, absence of incentives inadequate training of instructors the temporary nature of supervisors appointments, absence of institutions exclusively for women in rural areas, low attendance, level of male students and suitability of location as places for female adult learners. The main drawback, were library facilities, irregular and inadequate supply of learning materials.

Bhatnagar, R. (1985) revealed that (1) most girls preferred to study in the afternoon or evening and wanted that, besides subjects, practical knowledge of knitting, embroidery and home science and drawing should also be imparted (2) the girls wished there were Radio, the Television sets and film shows at the centres, (3) the parents opined that there should proper arrangements for electricity, water, dresses and midday meals, (4) the instructors felt the need of teaching materials, small reading rooms and newspapers.

Sivarajan, N.K. (1985) concluded that (a) most of the respondents were aware of the pitiable social and educational conditions of Harijans and of the attempts at improving their lot, (b) inappropriate home condition and lack of motivation were two major factors affecting the education of Harijans, (c) the major reasons of attributed to the phenomenon of the dropping-out were: looking after the younger once in the family, helping parents, in household affairs and in their job etc. (d) economic backwardness was identified as the major constraints in obtaining literacy, (e) most of the Harijan population was concentrated near paddy fields, slums and colonies and the atmosphere was not conducive to education.

Srivastava, L.R.N and Gupta, B.S. (1985) in their study on methods, process and practices of non-formal education programme for Tribe students, found that getting the community cooperation was not attempted by the teachers. The centres covered under this study had not provided any specially prepared instructional material.

Murthy, S.K. (1986) stated that there was a centralized system of distribution of teaching learning materials to the centres. Lack of transport facilities in case of supervisors handicapped their supervisory work because the centres were located far and wide in blocks.

Nanipantulu, J.C. (1986) found that (1) the centres were working satisfactory with respect to class management, regularity and punctuality of instructors and learners, involvement of community, availability of resource material, organization of cocurricular activi ties, (2) the performance of girls of the general population and Scheduled Castes was good while that of the Scheduled Tribe girls was satisfactory.

Rajyalakshmi (1986) in her study found that (1) warming and playing materials were not available in all the centres because they were not supplied to any non-formal education centre. (2) Engagement in the household work, getting exhausted due to day-to-day work, family problems, ill-health, migration to another village, looking after children, feeling people, were some of the reasons for dropping out from the Non-Formal Education Centres.

Yadappanvar, A.V. (1994) found that (1) the learners expressed that inconvenience due to location of centres (28%) near roadside and frequent running buses, further caused inconvenience to them, (2) insufficient lighting at the centres (hurricane laterns). Further he concluded that there is an urgent need for the establishment and development of women's organizations at grass root level. They can play significant role in the education of women, attendance and learners achievement is positively and significantly related. The studies of Hebsur (1981), Laxminarayana (1982) and Rao (1983) have also established the above fact.

(c) Studies on Adult Education related to Scheduled Tribes

Srivastava (1969) in his study revealed that due to technological backwardness, educational development had been difficult to achieve among the tribal community. He also observed that the incidence of dropout was very high and attendance in the adult education classes was extremely low. The teachers needed more facilities to work effectively and efficiently. He pointed out that the high percentage of illiteracy makes it difficult to introduce and implement the development programmes.

Lakra (1976) studied the impact of adult education on the tribals of Ranchi District in Bihar. The main objective of the study was to investigate into the damages that had occurred in the socio-economic and political spheres of life of the tribals due to adult education imparted to them. He found that the standard of living rose with level of education which made them free from poverty, ignorance, social taboos and superstition. Gradually the tribals became educationally conscious an sent their children to schools. They became politically conscious and fused their several associations Adivasi Maha Sabha.

Haragopal (1979) in his study of two adult education centres in Warangal District of Andhra Pradesh found the reasons for the success of one adult education centre in Lambada Village. Initially the response was good but the enthusiasm decreased over a period of time and generally attendance thinned, finally culminating in the closure of the centre. The reasons were (1) Trooping of children into adult education centres and view of parents that education is for children and not for them; (2) the weak financial position of the sponsoring organization; (3) failure on the part of instructor to converse in their language with tribal learners; (4) the disinterest of the learners. The study further pointed out that centres were opened without proper planning. The study concluded that effective survey would have eliminated the crowding of children in one area. Thus, the study emphasizes the need for comprehensive planning before starting adult education centres.

Bastia (1982) studied the NAEP in the tribal regions of Orissa. The major findings were (1) deficiency in physical facilities at the centre, dearth of qualified instructors from the tribal community, in irrelevant instructional methods and materials, irregular payment to instructors, infrequent supervision of centres and lack of coordination among different agencies of Government. Further, the study revealed that impact of NAEP on neo-literates with regard to their functional development in terms of agricultural improvement was found to be negligible; and follow up programmes could not be organized effectively because of inadequate learning materials and library facilities.

Lakshminarayana (1984) in his study found that (1) the participants could not attend classes due to hard work and health problem; (2) 82.27 per cent of the participants were facing clothing and agricultural problems and (3) as many as 2.49 per cent expressed the problems of lack of reading and writing materials in the centres.

Neelam Avasthy (1986) studied the causes of illiteracy among the tribals and non-tribals in the Patha region of Uttar Pradesh. He found that dissatisfaction with contents of the courses conducted at the adult education centres, economic backwardness besides certain otherfactors, as the predominant reasons for keeping away from the centres.

Saha, Dutta Roy and Rajak (1991) conducted study on National Adult Education Programme in tribal village of Ranchi District in Bihar. They found that non-participation NAEP was due to lack of time, distance of adult education centres from house, busy with household activities or seeking jobs to earn their livelihood.

Vengaiah (2001) identified the continuing education needs of the tribal women attending the continuing education centres organized in Chitoor district of Andhra Pradesh. The study reveals that the tribal women would like to know more on first aid snake bite, welfare hostels for tribal students, fees concessions. reservation in education system, first aid to scorpion bite, self-employment trainings, tribal cooperative societies, ICDS Centres, family planning, education for the development, schemes for the development of tribals, AIDS, health insurance scheme, employment generating programmes, agricultural loans, first aid for injuries. DWCRA facilities for education of the tribes, contiguous diseases and Banjaras.

Sreekumar (1993) observed two things in the implementation of adult education programme in Kerala. First delay in the distribution of study material to the interior centres of the district, lack of communication and transportation. Another hindrance faced by implementing agency is the difficulty in changing the location of the adult education centres due to natural calamities like heavy monsoon. local clashes.

The review of the related literature clearly shows that not much effort has been made in research to understand the problems faced by tribal women in their pursuit of education. Further, available studies are target based and programme oriented. Hence, there is a need to go deeper into the other aspects of education of women among the tribes so that efforts can be made to remove the obstacles. The knowledge will be helpful for the trainers to equip the field function in their job effectiveness by enhancing the maximization women's participation in adult literacy programmes and in raising the enrolment rate of the girls in formal schools.

Keeping in view the above an attempt was made to study the factors affecting the literacy rate among the primitive tribal woman. The literacy rate among the primitive tribal women of Kerala was found to be high and low in the case of A.P. Because of their Savara in Vizianagaram District of Andhra Pradesh and Cholanaickan and Kattunaickans of Kerala State have been selected.

In the case of Kerala, the Cholanaickan and Kattunaickan groups are found to be more or less comparable to the Savaras of A.P. in terms of primitiveness and degree of underdevelopment. Both Savara and Cholanaickan are declared as most primitive tribes by the Government of India while Kattunaickan has not been, still it is considered primitive. In view of the above, it was decided to study the above three groups of tribes to bring out the factors promoting, and inhibiting the spread of literacy among the tribes.

The pace of growth of literacy among the primitive tribal women has been very slow and uneven. The reasons attributed for this situation are many and complex. Some of the important reasons are structural factors like early marriages, children being employed in economic activities etc. Lacunae in the existing educational supporting services also adds to this problem. Further, lack of adequate consciousness among the older generation for the need of formal education also aggravates the situation. Poor economic conditions necessitate the contribution of every member of the family, the young and the old towards sustaining the family. Children of school going age are either looking after their young siblings in the family or en gaged in rearing the cattle or in some other economic activity. There are many personal and family reasons forcing a number of tribal girls to discontinue their education midway. Attainment of puberty and getting ready for marriage, meager employment opportunities for women are a few reasons for not attending the school. It was rightly said that if a man is made literate he himself benefits and if a woman is made literate the entire family benefits. Keeping this in view high priority is accorded in educating the tribal women through non-formal and adult education programmes.

The literacy scenario of the country shows that its spread is uneven, varies from group to group, region to region and state to state. For instance, the tribal population of Andhra Pradesh is the largest (42 lakhs) in the Southern State of India with a literacy rate of 17.16 per cent. Whereas in the case of Kerala the tribal population is only 3.21 lakhs with a literacy rates of 57.22 per cent. On the other hand, Tamil Nadu and Karanataka States have 5.74 and 1.92 lakhs of total population with a literacy rate of 27.89 per cent and 36.01 per cent respectively. The trends in tribal population and rate of literacy shows that it differs from state to state with Kerala having highest rate of tribal literacy and the Andhra Pradesh lowest. A huge gap exists between Kerala and Andhra Pradesh in the literacy rate of tribal women. While it is 51.07% among the tribes of Kerala, it is 17.16% among the tribes of Andhra Pradesh. The knowledge of causative factor for this variation would enable the development agencies to address the educational problems of the tribes in a better way.

Factors contributing towards the promotion of literacy among primitive tribal women of Kerala and the factors inhibiting the same among the tribal women and tribal communities as a whole in Andhra Pradesh will be the pointers for the planners and administrators of tribal development to restructure the existing educational programmes by removing the inhibiting factors to make the programmes more effective.

Thus a systematic approach is needed in this regard. The present study envisages to make an in depth analysis of the factors affecting and contributing to the promotion of literacy among primitive tribal women with the following specific objectives:

OBJECTIVES

1. To find out the socio-economic and cultural background of primitive tribes.

2. To perceive the socio-economic and cultural factors inhibiting the promotion of literacy among the primitive tribes.

3. To examine the problems associated with the literacy among the primitive tribal women.

4. To study the factors contributing for the growth of literacy among the primitive tribal women.

5. To review on going developmental programmes with emphasis on the promotion of literacy among primitive tribal women.

6. To evolve appropriate strategies for the promotion of literacy among the primitive tribal women.

METHODOLOGY

Locale of the Study

Since the study is a comparative one, the tribal areas of the States of Andhra Pradesh and Kerala constitute the locale of the study. The primitive tribes chosen for the study are Savara of Andhra Pradesh and Cholanaickan and Kattunaickan of Kerala. In Andhra Pradesh, the Savara tribe is mostly inhabiting the Vizianagaram District in the mandals of Kurupam, G.L. Puram and G.M.Valasa. All these mandals are located in Eastern Ghats. Savara tribe was selected because it is not only one of the primitive tribes but also has a long historical background.

In the case of Kerala, among the promotive tribes Cholanaickans and Kattunaickans are selected in view of their backwardness in terms of literacy and nature of habitation. Majority of the population of these two tribes are inhibiting the Western Ghats of Kerala especially in the district of Malappuram. To be specific the locale of the study are Vizianagaram and Malappuram districts of Andhra Pradesh and Kerala respectively.

Size of the Sample

As the study is intended to identify the factors affecting the literacy rate among the primitive tribal women, it was decided to choose 10 habitations having majority of families from selected tribe from each state and from each habitation, all the tribal households were contacted to elicit the information required for the study. Total 20 habitations, 10 habitations from each state were selected in the second stage of sample selection. In the third stage, all the women of the households in the habitations were contacted. Thus, the total sample contacted comes to 278, of them 165 women are from A.P. and 113 women are from Kerala. In addition to the above, 80 school going girls and 53 school dropout were also studied. The total sample of 411 includes women,, and girls from both the states.

Tools used in the Study

The aim of the study is to identify the factors contributing for the promotion of literacy and socio-economic and cultural factors inhibiting the same. In addition, it is also intended to identify the problems associated wtih the growth of literacy among primitive tribal women. Keeping in view of the above, a schedule was constructed covering the aspects promoting and inhibiting literacy and problems associated with it. The schedule was designed in such a way that information could be obtained from four categories of the sample namely, married illiterate women, married literate women, school going girls and dropout girls. In addition, unstructured interviews along with observation were also carried out.

Data Collection

As the tribal habitations are located in the interior parts of the forests and most of the tribals are illiterate, speak only their own dialect, it was decided to hire the services of the people who are well-known to these groups and capable of communicating with them effectively. In the case of Savara, services of five interpreters hailing from the tribal areas were hired. In the case of Kerala, the services of part-time social workers employed by the ITDA of Nilambur in Malappuram district Kerala were hired. These social workers come from local tribes appointed by the Government of Kerala to act as intermediaries between the Government and the tribes.

Analysis of the Data

Data has been analysed at several levels, like, married literate women, married illiterate women, dropouts, school going girls, the position of heads of the families etc. Further a number of variables have been considered.

CHAPTER - II

SOCIO-ECONOMIC AND CULTURAL BACKGROUND OF THE TRIBES

"Tribes have always been sentimentally attached to the forests and considered them to be nature's gift. Their folklore is full of references to the forest. There are several rites and rituals related to some forest produce or the other. Many of the leaves, climbers etc., needed in magico-religious rites are procured from these forests. Many trees in the forests are considered to be abode of deities and are worshipped as such." (Ministry of Home Affairs, 1982, p.23).

I. CHOLANAICKANS

The name Cholanaickan first appeared in the book '*Tribes and Castes of Southern India*' by Thurston in 1909. He too did not talk about this group afterwards. The writers like Iyer, Louis, Ayyappan etc., who heavily depended on Thurston's work also failed to identify the existence of this tribe. Due to this reason Cholanaickan was unknown to the world till 1973. A journalist by chance had come across this group and exposed them to the outer world.

A community living in the Nilambur valley of the Malappuram district of Kerala, the Cholanaickans call themselves as Malanaickan. They recall their migration from the neighbouring forest areas of Karnataka. The community's name is derived from the words *cola* or *sola* meaning forest, and naickan meaning king, that is, the king of the forest. Among themselves, they speak a dialect of Kannada, which bears the influence of Tamil and Malayalam languages. A few of them speak Malayalam with outsiders. The Cholanaickan eat the meat of wild deer, bison, monkey, wild fowl, etc. Rice is a recent addition to their diet. They consume plenty of roots and tubers.

Appearance

The skin colour of Cholanaickan varies from dark brown to pale brown. They are well built but of short stature. Their hair is black and curly. The face is found or oval in shape with slightly developed zygomatic bones and supra orbital ridges. The occlusion pattern is edge to edge bite. Their teeth are comparatively small and have no diseases or cement coating at all. The nasal root is depressed and the nasal bridge is medium and the nasal profile is usually straight. The thickness of the lips vary from thin to medium. The above mentioned characteristics are recorded primarily on the basis of somatological observations.

Dress

Men of the Cholanaickan cover the portion from waist to knee of their body by a piece of cloth measuring two and half feet length and one-and-a-half feet in width and use a long doti to cover the upper body. Women wear a white cloth measuring four to six yards in length the one to two yards in width. They usually twist it around their waist and allow a portion of it to pass over the upper arm pit. In the past, before coming into contact with the outsiders, they did not cover the upper portion of their body. The practice of using leaves and barks for covering genital parts was given up when clothes became available to them from outside. The dresses are made of cotton and are available at the Tribal Development Department and Girijan Cooperative Society. Now most of them wear coloured lungi and bed sheets as these two items are issued to them through the development department. The State Government launched a development programme in 1976 and through this each household is given a set of clothes and aluminium vessels. Clothing pattern does not indicate any social, political and economic status in the Cholanaickan society.

Ornaments

Cholanaickan wear bangles made of grass. The bangle in their dialect is called Ullu bale. This bangle is made out of a special kind of dried grass artistically twisted and joined by a knot. The grass when dried gives a golden colour and the colour never fades even after a long wear and tear. The Cholanaickan women usually wear these bangles on the upper arm just above the elbow. More that half a dozen bangles are worn in one hand itself. Now-a-days they wear necklaces of beads and aluminium rings purchased from Nilambur market. They make rings with 20 and 25 paise coins and wear them on the fingers.

Distribution

There are ten territorial groups (Janmom) among the Cholanaickan, and each group is kinship-based. Karimpuzha, Panapuzha, Taalipuzha, Kuppan Mala, Pooch Appara, Kormpuzha, Maniakkadavu, Alakkal, Ambilimala and Olikkatodu are the ten identified clans.

Nomadism, Kin Group, Territory and Janmom Rights

Descent is traced by the Cholanaickans through a particular Alai (cave). Therefore the households belonging to one kin group has a well-defined territory over which the members have exclusive socio-political and economic rights and special claim for hunting, gathering and collection of minor forest produce. The territory over which a kin group wields its rights and privileges is called Janmom. Those belonging to a particular kin group generally do not trespass and encroach upon the Janmom rights of another. Sometimes, violation of this customary right results in violent quarrels leading to bloodshed. Sometimes, they stay in the upper valley during summer months for better collection of forest produce, The hamlets are distributed in three contiguous areas of the Nilambur Forest Division, viz., Meenmutti and Tailpuzha (Karulai Range), Punchakolli (Chungathara Range) and Chaliyar (Chungathara Range).

Janmom (Territories)

The Cholanaickans who number about 350 inhabit the mountain ranges of Nilambur. They live in caves (alai). Each 'alai' is a kin group hamlet. Households belonging to a kin group tend to congregate at a particular 'alai'. The Cholanaickans though living in a scattered rocky caves in the interior forests, are always found on the banks of rivers. Although their homes are alais, they wander about from one place to another in search of a wide variety of berries, roots and tubers, nuts, honey, peach, leaves and many other minor forest produce, In fact, they lead a nomadic life throughout the year except for the rainy season. "They subsist on vegetable food and gather forest products for barter" (Mathur, 1977).

Nomadism

Usually the Cholanaickans stay in one place for three to five days and then move on as the food supply becomes scarce in the surroundings. Their movements cannot be explained in simple economic terms. Apart from the availability of food, there are four essential features which are responsible for their movements. The first is that the caves give them protection during the monsoons when rivers are in spate. Secondly, they move to another cave because it give them protection from wild beasts. Thirdly, they move from one cave to another as they burry the dead in their own caves. The settlement is extremely limited in size. Each cave houses form one to three conjugal families. These families constitute a kin group. Each family is a distinct economic unit. Finally, the Cholanaickans are habitually nomadic. The necessity for collaboration in subsistence activities is essentially a function of division of labour as conceived and practised by the Cholanaickans. Male and females must depend on each other, for each sex is trained in certain works.

Hunting and Fishing

Cholanaickans hunt in all months except in rainy season. Hunting in a group, they use dogs and small nets made of ropes. The net is suitably located with the help of trees and sticks and beat is made towards the net. Any animal caught in the net is killed with axe (Kodeli). The important animals they hunt are iguana, hogdeer and monkey. They train their dogs to chase wild bear or big deer and also to catch small deer and rabbits.

The most interesting method of catching fish employed is the use of "poison". It is widely practiced by the Cholanaickans. For poison they use a concoction of the bark of Ingal tree, when the fish are stupefied by the poison and float on the surface of the water they are caught by hand. Rod and line is also practiced, the hook being home made, a piece of bent iron.

Division of Labour

Hardly ever does a member of one sex intrude into the sphere of the other. Each sex has its own way of bearing burdens—men gather exclusively the main forest produce like honey, pepper and seeds as well as dammer, while women cooperate with the men in the collection of other minor forest produce such as cardamom, ginger, turmeric etc. In basket making cooking, child rearing and other household work men cooperate with women.

Children participate in hunting and food gathering. Even old people are found going for hunting and food gathering activities.

Ritual factors also play their part in defining the respective roles of men and women. The priests are invariably men while midwives are women.

Family Structure

The primitive Cholanaickans family is based on individualism and does not represent in any way the joint family system of the Hindus. When a grown up son marries, he separates from his parents and establishes a new family. The nuclear Cholanaickan family consists of the male head, his wife (or wives) and unmarried children. Basically Cholanaickans family is nuclear in nature but some time it may consists of one or two additional members. The Cholanaickan are a patrilineal people and as such, the families are patrilineal and partrilocal. Father is the head of the family. His is the supreme authority in family affairs.

After marriage, the wife goes to live in husband's alai though this is the general rule, yet 10 cases of resident sons-in-law were found who live in the caves of their fathers-in-law. In such cases succession and inheritance passes through female line.

It is also a general rule that the girls marry at an earlier age than boys but after their puberty. The Cholanaickans have very little idea about their age. They calculate their age by their physical appearance and capacity to go for hunting and food gathering.

Matrilateral cross cousin marriages are practiced. But patrilineal and parallel cousin marriages are forbidden. However, it has been noticed an instance of parallel cousin marriage which has been looked down upon by the elders. A man can marry his deceased brother's wife (junior levirate and senior levirate) or his wife's younger sister (sororate). A Cholanaickan man is not allowed to marry his deceased wife's elder sister. They are not also allowed to choose their mates within the blood relationship of any kind. Bride price (Kana Ana) is compulsory.

Endogamy

The Cholanaickans is an endogamous group, marriage outside their tribe is prohibited.

Exogamy

Members marry generally outside their Alai. They consider that members living in an Alai are related by blood. Thus each Alai is an exogamous unit (Kudumba). Hence, marriage within the Alai is prohibited. Divorce is very rarely practiced in this cummunity

Social Control

Janmakkaran is the head of an Alai. He is responsible for managing the affairs of the tribe in the Alai. He officiates as the priest for death and marriage ceremonies and presides over magical practices. His permission is required for marriage and burying the dead. His post is hereditary. The Cholanaickans do not have a common tribal council for the whole community and as such there is no common authority to deal with different social ceremonial and religious matters

Religion

The Cholanaickans worship Mala Daivam (Jungle God) and ancestor spirits. A bell metal idol of an elephant with a mahout on its back is propitiated by them. During the monsoon this idol is brought from an unknown cave in the interior jungle and installed in a sacred corner of the cave into which women are prohibited to enter. Special Pujas are conducted by them during this period. As soon as the monsoon is over the deity is taken back to its original cave. Each Alai possesses an idol of Mala Daivam and it is the responsibility of Janmakkaran to bring the deity to the cave from the forest and take it back to its original place.

The Cholanaickans also propitiate their ancestral spirits. They believe that the dead ancestors (males and females) will protect them from the evil influence of lesser spirits. When illness occures in a family, prayers are offered and special vows are made to them. Gourds are waved over patients uttering mantras for curing the illness. Boiled rice, tobacco, betel leaves are the main offerings given to them as well as to their God.

Life Cycle

There are no special puberty rites and rituals among the Cholanaickans. However, a woman after these events is secluded for four days in one corner of the cave. She is not allowed to touch the cooking utensils. On the fifth day she takes bath and resumes her normal household work. The bath on the fifth day after puberty is called Neeratal. During the menstruation period, which is called "thinka" woman is supposed to be unclean. She is not permitted to do household work. On the third day or fourth day when the menstruation period is over, she takes bath and resumes her normal household work. During her monthly period sexual activity is prohibited.

Birth

When labour pain starts a midwife (Othachi) is called into attend the expectant woman. Generally the wife of the tribal chief acts as a midwife. Traditionally the Cholanaickan had no separate place of confinement but at present a separate temporary shed of bamboo and leaves are constructed for delivery. Women is secluded in this hut for 40 days. The midwife is paid in kind. The child is bathed by Othachi. The mother is bathed for 40 days in hot water. The midwife cuts the umbilical cord.

No name giving ceremony is performed among the Cholanaickans but a name is selected by the Janmakkaran from the mother's line. Generally a child is named at the age of 8 or 10 years.

Death

The Cholanaickans bury the dead. They dig a shallow grave, about waist deep and the deceased is buried with the head towards west. They have their own burial ground. The belongings of the deceased are generally buried with the dead. It is the responsibility of Janmakkaran of each Alai to arrange the funeral procession and dig grave. For funeral minimum seven persons are required. The wife of the deceased accompanies the funeral procession to the burial ground. Without the permission of Janmakkaran the body cannot be buried. The bereaved member will not go for food gathering for 3 days.

The Cholanaickans conduct obsequies after a month or so when resources are available. The Janmakkaran officiates as the priest. The kin supply rice, roots and tubers for conducting death rites.

They conduct this ceremony either on Tuesday or Wednesday but depending upon the availability of the resources. Janmakkaran used a bark turban in olden days. Now-a-days a cotton head gear is used. Janmakkaran, consanguines and affines are fed at night. The cooked rice is placed in a leaf for the dead. The kin and Janmakkaran dance around the leaf throughout the night. On the following morning the janmakkaran eats the rice. In another leaf boiled rice is placed in the morning and the dead is propitiated by the Janmakkaran. This rice is also eaten by the priest after the worship. All other dead ancestors are also worshipped on this day, by giving the offerings of rice, fish curry and pepper.

II. KATTUNAICKAN

The term Kattunaickan has been derived from the word 'Kadu', meaning forest and naiackan, meaning leader or headman. The Kattunaickans are one of the primitive tribal communities of Kerala. Ethnographic accounts reveal that they once inhabited Calicut region. Now they are mainly distributed in the Wayanad district of Kerala. Their natural environment is characterized by hilly terrain, high altitude, low humidity, thick forest and high rainfall. They have their own dialect, Within the is close to the Dravidian language of Kannada. Within the family, they use their dialect and the regional language Malayalam to converse with the people form outside. Malayalam script is used for writing. Tatto marks and the attire of their females make the members of this community distinguishable. They are non-vegetarians and eat pork. Rice and ragi are their staple cereals. They consume milk and milk products. Coconut oil is the medium of cooking. Men occasionally consume alcoholic drinks.

Settlement Pattern

The Kattunaickan settlements are seen distributed both inside the forests and also in revenue lands. A Kattunaickan settlement is known as 'Kudi'. The average number of households in a hamlet is 10.6. The maximum number of houses found in a hamlet is 22 and the Minimum 4. Some of the present large sized Kattunaickans hamlets are colonies particularly created by the Department of Forest by bringing Kattunaickan families from different hamlets. Because of the propinquity to the forest, the Kattunaickan could maintain their traditional forest oriented economic life. The Kattunaickans of most of the hamlets are not in a position to state the exact extent of land in their possession. However, a few families are found cultivating ginger, plantain and vegetables in their household plots.

Housing

The Kattunaickans are found benefited by various housing schemes: 60 per cent of the families are living in Government built tiled or asbestos roofed houses. The household articles are meagre. Usually they sleep on mats made of grass.

Demographic Particulars

The average family size of the Kattunaickans is 4.01%. Their sex ratio is 10:16. The child population constitute 37.6 per cent which shows the existence of a large number of dependants in the society. There are 6.8 per cent married men between the ages of 15 to 19 and 29.4 per cent married women in the age group of 15 to 19, which shows that the Kattunaickans marry at an early age compared to the general population. Further, it may be said that women are married at an early age than the men. Kattunaickans are divided into clans. Marriage with the father's sister's daughter and the mother's brother's daughter is permissible. Marriage types in this tribe consists of marriage by capture, service, elopement, exchange and negotiation. Monogamy is the norm and sororal polygamy is also practice. Badge (thali), vermilion, bangles, finger-and-toe rings and nose-studs are the symbols of marriage. Bride price is paid in cash and the patrilocal rule of residence is followed. Divorce is permissible with social approval and barrenness can be one of the reasons for it. Either the husband or the wife can seek divorce and the children can be the liability of either parent. Widows, widowers and divorcees are allowed to remarry. Nuclear and vertically extended types of families are found among them. The descent pattern is patrillineal and the eldest son is the successor. Women have different roles to perform in agriculture, fishing, collection of fuel, fetch ing of potable water and in social affairs. The naming ceremony and puberty rites are observed in the community. Marriage rituals are performed at the brides residence and a feast is hosted by the brides' parents. The dead are cremated and the remains are disposed off in hill streams. Death pollution and ancestor worship are observed.

Occupation

Food gathering, hunting, fishing and trapping of birds and animals are the traditional occupations of Kattunaickans, but, today only a few of them pursue these occupations. A few of them are landowning cultivators. Majority of them are agricultural labourers. Child labour exists among them. Social control is maintained through a traditional Council headed by a Mudali. Cash fine is imposed for violating traditional norms and insulting the Council.

Religion

Kattunaickans are animists combined with animatism. They worship trees, rocks, the sun, the moon, the deities of Bhairava, Masti, Mala Daivom and the spirits of their ancestors. Besides animism and animatism they also worship Hindu Gods and Goddesses. A Mudali or priest performs the rituals and protects the members from evil spirits. Festivals like Onam and Vishnu are celebrated. The community has oral traditions, folk-tales and folk-songs. Both men and women sing songs and take part in dances. Percussion instruments are played by them.

Education

Among Kattunaickan mens literacy rate is 47.3 per cent and that of women is 40 per cent. This literacy is confined to the youth and school going children. Children belonging to interior hamlets are found not attending any school, not even balwadies and anganwadis. A number of children have dropped out from the school.

Family life

Kattunaickan woman enjoy respectable position in the family because she is capable of standing on her own legs. But the high frequency of desertions that are in vogue in the Kattunaickans' society adversely affects the women in a severe manner than the men. Even though both men and women are allowed to desert their spouses and remarry and number of times, it is often found that after certain age a woman is left alone in her house because of her inability to remarry. Usually such women are looked after by their grown up offspring or in their absence by their friendly neighbours. Widower remarriage is very large compared to the frequency of widow remarriages

Social Organisation

Kattunaickans in the past lead a nomadic life as bands in the forest. Now they are in the process of settling down in small sized hamlets. Head of the 'Padi' or hamlet is called 'Mooppan', but outsiders address him as 'Mothali'. Mooppan has an important role to play in all the religious and social functions of the hamlet. Very small sized hamlets do not have a Mooppan. On other occasions like puberty ceremony, child birth, illness and in other afflictions etc., the Mooppan acts as oracle. When a Mooppan dies the position is inherited by his younger brother and in the absence of any brother his eldest son would become the next Mooppan.

There is a sacred hut (sometimes more than one) in every hamlet called 'daivamana'. Except the Mooppan no one has access to 'daivamana'. Communal feast is organized during religious ceremonies. Only men are allowed to cook on these occasions.

Women in separation and the dependent children pose major social problems. But a notable aspect is that the female child is not discriminated in any walk of life. Even though males enjoy a superior status in the political and religious sphere both male and females play equal role in running the family.

Unlike the other tribal communities of Wayanad, among Kattunaickans there are very few instances of unwed mothers. The Kattunaickans marry at an early age. But desertions leading to divorce are significantly high. The reasons for broken families are excessive drinking, extra marital relations particularly of the husband neglect of family duties etc.

III SAVARAS

"The Aitareya Brahmana of Rigveda makes the Savaras the descendants of the sons of Viswamitra who were cursed to become impure by their father for an act of disobedience, while the Ramayana describes them as having emanated from the body of Vasista's Cow to fight against Viswamitra".

Savara is one of the important and ancient tribal group living in Srikakulam and Vizianagaram districts of Andhra Pradesh and this region spreads from forest and hill tracts of Srikakulam to Vizianagaram and Visakhapatnam districts and these hill range form part of Eastern Ghats.

Settlement Pattern

The Savaras construct their houses in two or three rows parallel to each other in a linear pattern. The houses are rectangular in shape, roof is thatched with sedge grass (dobba gaddi in regional language, Telugu) a kind of grass locally available. Walls are made of mud or plastered with mud. Almost every house consists two doors, one opening to the courtyard and the other to the backyard. Most of the villages are situated at the foothills and are single tribe villages. They generally live on hilltops or valleys and practice shifting cultivation.

Appearance on Dressing Pattern

The Savara believed to be the admixture of Mongolian and Dravidian stock with short to medium stature, long and high head; broad and small face with small flattened nose.

The dress of an adult male Savara consists of a 'gavancha' or 'gochi' and a thick coarse white bed sheet spread over the shoulders locally known as 'dukandi'. Women use sarees and they are not habituated to wearing blouse. They usually cover the upper part of the body with one end of the same saree. Children of below 12 years, boys wear only rags, shirts and shorts, girls wear skirt and jacket. Both men and women dress their hair regularly by applying coconut oil and combing.

Social Organisation

Lineage is called " Kulam Marangi". All the kulam marangi trace their descent to a common ancestor and all the members of a lineage are quite aware of their geneological relationship with each other. Nuclear family is common among them. The Savara family is characterized by patrilocal, patrilineal and patricentral.

Savaras have supreme faith in the spirits and deities, which are believed to guide their destiny. They believe that all the ailments are caused by the evil spirits where as good is done by benevolent ones. They worship mainly two deities namely, 'Sandhidemudu' and 'Jakaradevatha'. During the festivals and rituals, the families prepare special dishes and consume larger quantities of intoxicating drinks and dance throughout the night.

Social control is maintained by the village headman called 'Gamong' and a religious headman 'Buya'. Gamong assisted by Buya will organize all the economic activities, festivals and look after the law and order in the village.

Marriage by elopement, negotiation and capture are practiced. Bride price "Olilebu" or "Oli" is present in the community. Divorce is considerably easier to get by approaching the Tribal Council.

Generally, they eat food prepared by cooking 'Korralu' (Italian millet) with vegetable curry and gruel.

Mixed cropping is commonly practiced. After preparing the soil, they mix 'Korra' (Italian Millet), 'Ganti' or 'Bajra' (pearl millet), 'Janumu' (Jute) and 'Moonna' (Great Millet) and broad-cast them. Shifting cultivation has been the main source of livelihood for them due to lack of sufficient cultivable lands within their reach.

Division of Labour

Division of labour in this community depends on the age and sex. Men attend to the work of getting the land ready for cultivation, the women takes the responsibility of sowing, weeding and harvesting. The main responsibility of men is to hunt animals while women are responsible for the collection of minor forest produce.

Children take care of the younger siblings, collection of minor forest produce and cattle grazing, pig rearing, domestic work etc. Children entrusted with economic work find it difficult to enter into schools

Concerning the death rites, as soon as a person dies in a house, a gun, loaded with gun powder is fired at the door, or, if plenty of powder is available, several shots are fired, to frighten away the Kulba (spirit). Water is poured over the body while in an house. The only wood used for the pyre is that of the mango, and of Pongamia globra (Fawett, 1906).

Tribal Shandies

Shandies-the weekly market places play an important functional role in the socio-economic and cultural life of the tribal population Men, women and children of different age groups regularly attend these shandies. The shandies not only fulfil certain needs of the buyers and sellers, but also act as an agent of culture exchange. These are the occasions to meet their friends and relatives, exchange informations and also an occasion for young tribal boys and girls to meet each other sometimes leading to marriage. Shandy is also the the place to the Savaras and other tribes in Eastern Ghats to come into contact with modern consumer goods and other goods not known traditionally to them. Despite the forces of modernization and new technology knocking at their doors, Savaras continue to lag behind socially, economically and educationally.

CHAPTER - III

SOCIO-ECONOMIC PROFILE OF TRIBAL HEADS OF THE FAMILIES

In this chapter, an attempt is made to understand the socio-economic profile of the tribal heads of families in terms of their age, sex and education etc. Understanding of the socio-economic profile of the heads of the families is necessary, since the management of the families and the members depend on the heads of the families which has a bearing on the attitude of the heads as well as members towards education.

(i) Sex-wise Distribution of the Heads of the Families of the Sample

The sample for the study altogether from Savaras, Kattunaickan and Cholanaickan consists of 278 families. Following table provides infromation on the sex-wise distribution of the heads of the families.

TABLE 1

Sex-wise distribution of the heads of the selected tribal families

S.No.	Sex	Tribe			Total
		Savara	Kattunaickans	Cholanaickans	
1.	Men	110 (66.67)	64 (65.98)	14 (87.50)	88 (67.63)
2.	Women	55 (33.33)	33 (34.02)	2 (12.50)	90 (32.37)
Total		**165 (100.00)**	**97 (100.00)**	**16 (100.00)**	**278 (100.00)**

The sex and tribewise classification presented in Table 1 shows that nearly one-third of the families are headed by the men. The trend is similar in the case of all the three tribes. Majority of the women, heading the families are either widows or divorced.

(ii) Age-wise Distribution of the Heads of the Families

Information presented in Table 2 shows that 9 families are headed by the people whose age is 20 years. About 7.19 percent of the families are headed by the elder generation of more that 61 years of age. It is also clear that majority of the families are headed by the people falling in the age group of 21-50 years. Similar trend is noticed in all the three tribes. It is interesting to note that majority of the heads of families come from younger age groups.

TABLE 2

Age-wise distribution of the heads of the selected tribal families

S. No.	Age (yrs.)	Savaras Men	Savaras Women	Kattunaickans Men	Kattunaickans Women	Cholanaickans Men	Cholanaickans Women	Total
1.	<20	6 (5.45)	1 (1.82)	1 (1.56)	0 (0.00)	0 (0.00)	1 (50.00)	9 (3.24)
2.	21-30	38 (34.55)	16 (29.09)	19 (29.69)	12 (36.36)	3 (21.43)	1 (50.00)	89 (32.01)
3.	31-40	31 (28.18)	20 (36.36)	15 (23.44)	8 (24.24)	8 (57.14)	0 (0.00)	82 (29.50)
4.	41-50	20 (18.18)	9 (16.36)	11 (17.19)	9 (27.27)	1 (7.14)	0 (0.00)	50 (10.07)
5.	51-60	11 (10.00)	6 (10.91)	9 (14.06)	1 (3.03)	1 (7.14)	0 (0.00)	20 (7.19)
6.	61>	4 (3.64)	3 (5.45)	9 (14.06)	3 (9.09)	1 (7.14)	0 (0.00)	20 (7.19)
Total		**110 (100.00)**	**55 (99.99)**	**64 (100.00)**	**33 (100.00)**	**14 (100.00)**	**2 (100.00)**	**278 (100.00)**

(iii) Tribe and Sex-wise Occupational Status of the Heads of Families

In order to identify the major occupations and source of livelihood of the tribal families, occupational categories of heads of the families among the three tribes are given below.

TABLE 3
Distribution of heads of families according to tribe, sex and occupation

S. No.	Occupation	Tribe: Savaras Men	Savaras Women	Kattunaickans Men	Kattunaickans Women	Cholanaickans Men	Cholanaickans Women	Total
1.	Cultivation	109 (99.09)	51 (92.73)	51 (79.69)	22 (66.67)	0 (0.00)	0 (0.00)	233 (85.35)
2.	Minor forest products	0 (0.00)	0 (0.00)	0 (0.00)	4 12.12)	11 (78.57)	2 (100.00)	17 (2.16)
3.	Plantation	0 (0.00)	4 (7.27)	0 (0.00)	0 (0.00)	2 (14.29)	0 (0.00)	5 (1.83)
4.	Agriculture labour	1 (0.91)	0 (0.00)	1 (1.35)	0 (0.00)	1 (7.14)	0 (0.00)	2 (0.72)
5.	Cleaner	0 (0.00)	0 (0.00)	2 (3.13)	0 (0.00)	0 (0.00)	0 (0.00)	2 (0.72)
6.	Labour	0 (0.00)	0 (0.00)	11 (17.19)	7 (21.21)	0 (0.00)	0 (0.00)	18 (6.47)
	Total	**110 (100.00)**	**55 (99.99)**	**64 (99.99)**	**33 (100.00)**	**14 (100.00)**	**2 (100.00)**	**278 (99.99)**

Information presented in Table 3 shows that 85.35 per cent of the heads of families are mainly engaged in cultivation. This applies to the Savara and Kattunaickan Tribes. Collection of minor forest produce come next in importance. But, majority of Cholanaickan depend on the collection of minor forest produce followed by plantation. Similar trend is noticed among the Cholanaickan women heads of the families. It is interesting to note that even among the women heads of families the major occupation is cultivation followed by the collection of minor forest produce.

(iv) Educational Background of the Heads of the Families

Tribal heads of the families are classified into different groups based on their level of education. The classification reveals that 56.83 per cent of the head of the families are illiterate and about 40 per cent are educated upto primary level. Only 3.96 per cent of the tribal heads of the families are educated upto high school level. The tribe-wise and sex-wise classification shows that among Savara men, the percentage of illiterate (48.18) is equal to that of those who have completed their primary education (48.18). It is interesting to note that among Savara heads of families more or less women compete (3.64%) with the men heads of families at the level of high school studies, four men have completed high school studies while 3 women have completed the same (5.45%).

TABLE 4

Distribution of heads of the families by education, tribe and sex

S. No.	Level of Education	Savaras Men	Savaras Women	Kattunaickans Men	Kattunaickans Women	Cholanaickans Men	Cholanaickans Women	Total
1.	Illiterates	53 (48.18)	37 (67.27)	43 (67.18)	17 (51.52)	7 (50.00)	1 (50.00)	158 (56.83)
2.	Primary	53 (48.18)	15 (27.27)	19 (20.69)	14 (42.42)	7 (50.00)	1 (50.00)	109 (39.21)
3.	High School	4 (3.64)	3 (5.45)	2 (3.12)	2 (6.06)	0 (0.00)	0 (0.00)	11 (3.96)
	Total	**110 (100.00)**	**55 (99.99)**	**64 (99.99)**	**33 (100.00)**	**14 (100.00)**	**2 (100.00)**	**278 (100.00)**

In the case of Kattunaickan nearly two thirds of heads of families are illiterates, one-third of them are educated upto primary level and only two of them are educated upto high school level. Among women, half of them are illiterate and rest of them are educated upto primary level except 2 who have crossed to high school. On the whole, majority of the family heads are illiterate. Whereas in the case of Cholanaickan half of the heads of families are illiterate

Whereas in the case of Cholanaickan half of the heads of families are illiterate and the rest of the household heads are literates upto primary level. Even in the case of women headed families the same trend prevails.

Above description of the background of the heads of the families shows that two-thirds of the families headed by men and one-third by women. Majority of them are less than 40 yeas of age with cultivation as their main occupation with low literacy.

CHAPTER - IV

SOCIO-ECONOMIC AND CULTURAL PROFILE OF THE TRIBAL WOMEN

Primitive tribes mostly depend on hunting, food gathering and cultivation for their livelihood and live in remote areas, deep inside the forest. Their exposure to the outside world is minimum and mainly occurs on shandy days. Government, Non-Governmental Agencies and Missionaries have made some efforts to modernize these tribes by providing education and feeding the information about the outside world. All these efforts have resulted in raising the literacy rate among the tribes from 11.30 per cent in 1971 to 29.50 per cent in 1991. In case of women thė growth of literacy is very low i.e., only 4.85% to 18.19% from 1971 to 1991. However, it appears that the growth of literacy in Kerala among the primitive tribal groups is more than the primitive tribes in Andhra Pradesh. In order to understand the factors facilitating and inhibiting the growth of literacy among the women in primitive tribes an attempt in this chapter is made to analyse the socio-economic and cultural background of the women among Savara, Kattunaickan and Cholanaickan.

In order to identify the problems, promoters and inhibitors of literacy among women, information was collected from the women of different ages and marital status i.e, married illiterate women, married literate women, school going girls and dropout girls.

Women in tribal communities in India except in a few spheres of their life enjoy equal status with their men. Socially they are not looked down and participate in all the social activities along with the men. Further, divorce and widow remarriages are permitted. Though there is sexual division of labour, women's economic contribution is not less than that of their men. No doubt even in many of these communities due to their patrilinial nature, a tribal woman after her marriage takes up her residence with her husband. This means the labour of the woman after her marriage goes to her husband's household but not to her parents household. Internalization of this attitude by the girl's parents is one of the many reasons for neglecting the education of the girls.

(i) Women and their Level of Education

The sample women are divided into 4 groups such as illiterate married women, literate married women, dropout girls and school going girls. This information is presented in Table 5.

TABLE 5
Distribution of the sample women according to their literacy level

S. No.	Category	Savaras	Kattunaickans	Cholanaikans	Total
1.	Married Illiterate Women	132 (80.00)	74 (76.28)	8 (50.00)	214 (76.98)
2.	Married literate women	33 (20.00)	23 (23.72)	8 (50.00)	64 (2302)
*3.	School drop-out girls	64	16	----	80
*4.	School going girls	42	11	---	53

* These two categories have been dealt with in a separate section.

Table 5 indicates that 76.98 per cent of the married women in the sample families are illiterate and the remaining 23.02 per cent are literate married women. In the case of Savara 80.00 per cent of them were illiterate married women and 20.00 per cent are literate married women, whereas among Kattunaickans 76.28 per cent are illiterate married women and the rest 23.72 per cent are literate married women.

The above table also indicates that among Cholanaickans half of the sample women are married illiterates and the other half are married illiterates.

(ii) Marital practices among the Tribal Women

It is assumed that the tribal girls get married immediately after they attain puberty. Generally the girls among the tribes attain their first menarche between 11-15 years and if they are married of immediately after their first menarche, it is obvious as one assume that they have no chance to enroll themselves in the schools unless their parents agree to postpone the marriage.

(iii) Age at Marriage among the Illiterate Married Women

Table 6 give the tribe wise information about their age at marriage.

Among Savara women most of them (62.12%) got married before 15 years of age followed by 30.30 per cent between the ages of 16-20 years and 7.57 per cent of them have married between 21 to 35 years.

In the case of Kttunaickan 28.38 per cent of them got married between the ages of 11-15 years and 29.73 per cent of them got married between 16 to 20 years, surprisingly, 41.89 per cent of them got married between 21 to 35 years.

Whereas in the case of Cholanaickans, half of them got married between 11-15 year age. 37.50 per cent of the women got married between 16-20 years and rest of them (12.50%) between the age of 21-25 years.

TABLE 6
Distribution of sample illiterate married women according to their age at marriage

S. No.	Age Group (Years)	Savaras	Kattunaickans	Cholanaickans	Total
1.	11-15	82 (62.12)	21 (28.38)	4 (50.00)	107 (50.00)
2.	16-20	40 (30.30)	22 (29.73)	3 (37.50)	65 (30.37)
3.	21-25	4 (3.03)	14 (18.92)	1 (1.250)	19 (8.88)
4.	26-30	4 (3.03)	10 (13.51)	0 (0.00)	14 (6.54)
5.	31-35	2 (1.51)	7 (9.46)	0 (0.00)	9 (4.21)
	Total	**132 (99.99)**	**74 (100.00)**	**8 (100.00)**	**214 (100.00)**

In total 50 per cent of sample illiterate women are married before they attained 15 years of age. 30.37 per cent are married between 16 to 20 years. The rest of the sample illiterate women have got remarried between 21-35 years.

It is clear that if the first two age groups are clubbed the percentage of tribal women who are married young come to 80.37 and this indicates that due to their only marriage even if some of them are willing to enroll in the school, in all probability due to early marriages they could not do it.

(iv) Age at Marriage among Literate Married Women

Based on the age at marriage, the educated women belonging to the three tribal groups are classified into five groups. The classification shows that among Savara 42.42 per cent of educated women got married when they were below 15 years of age and 30.3 per cent of them got married between 16-20 years of age. About 27.85 per cent of them got married between 21 to 35 years. In the case of Kattunaickans, 83.86 per cent of them got married when they were below 20 years and rest of them got married after 20 years of age. In the case of Cholanaickans majority of them (75.00%) got married between the age of 16-20 years. Only 25.00 per cent of them got married below 15 years. On the whole, majority of the literate tribal women got married when they were below 20 years of age.

TABLE 7
Distribution of the sample literate married women according to their age at marriage

S No.	Age (Years)	Savara	Kattunaickans	Cholanaickans	Total
1.	11-15	14 (42.42)	1 (4.35)	2 (25.00)	24 (37.50)
2.	16-20	10 (30.30)	10 (43.48)	6 (75.00)	26 (40.62)
3.	21-25	4 (12.12)	9 (39.13)	0 (0.00)	8 (12.50)
4.	26-30	2 (6.06)	2 (8.69)	0 (0.00)	3 (4.69)
5.	31-35	3 (9.67)	1 (4.35)	0 (0.00)	3 (4.69)
	Total	**33 (100.00)**	**23 (100.00)**	**8 (100.00)**	**64 (100.00)**

Like the illiterate married tribal women, in this group also i.e., literate married women were married at an early age. It means that early marriage did not hinder these women to get enrolled in the schools unlike the illiterate married women. Further, enquiry revealed that the difference between these two groups of women is that in the case of literate married women, their parents were interested to send their daughters to school for a year or two before their marriage.

(v) Educational Background of the Family

In order to identify the extent of educational environment prevailing in the homes of the tribes for the promotion of girls education, the women were asked about their parents and siblings exposure to the education. The information shows that per cent of the women expressed that their fathers have education upto primary level. On the other hand 19.06 per cent of the women expressed that their mothers in their childhood were enrolled in primary schools. The rest of the women are not sure about the extent of their parents educational level.

In the case of siblings, 27.34 per cent of the women informed that their elder brothers, elder sister, younger brothers and younger sisters were educated upto primary level. In addition, 8.27 per cent of the women also disclosed that their sisters had attained secondary level of education.

Tribe-wise analysis shows that 24-24 per cent of women belonging to Savaras tribe revealed that their fathers were educated upto primary level, 19.39 per cent of them said that their mothers also had primary education. Among Kattunaickans 39.82 per cent of the women's fathers and 18.58 per cent of mothers were educated upto primary level. Further, 20.35 per cent of them also informed that their sisters were educated upto secondary level. As Cholanaickan women disclosed that they came from illiterate families, their information is presented in the table.

TABLE 8

Level of Education of the parents and Sibling of the Sample

S. No.	Relationship to the sample	Savaras (N = 165)			Total	Kattunaikans (N = 113)			Total	Total sample (N = 278)			Total
		Primary Education	Secondary Education	Not known		Primary Education	Secondary Education	Not known		Primary Education	Secondary Education	Not known	
1	Father	40 (24.24)	-	125 (75.75)	165 (99.99)	45 (39.82)	--	68 (60.18)	113 (100.00)	85 (30.58)	--	193 (69.42)	278 (100.00)
2.	Mother	32 (19.39)		133 (80.61)	165 (100.99)	21 (18.58)		92 (81.42)	113 (100.00)	53 (19.06)		225 (80.94)	278 (100.00)
3.	Elder brother	44 (26.67)		121 (73.33)	165 (100.99)	32 (28.32)		81 (71.68)	113 (100.00)	76 (27.34)		202 (72.66)	278 (100.00)
4.	Younger brother	31 (18.79)		134 (81.21)	165 (100.99)	15 (13.27)		98 (86.73)	113 (100.00)	50 (17.99)		228 (82.01)	278 (100.00)
5.	Elder sister	35 (21.21)		130 (78.79)	165 (100.99)	15 (13.27)	12 (10.62)	86 (76.11)	113 (100.00)	50 (17.99)	12 (4.31)	216 (77.78)	278 (100.00)
6.	Younger sister	25 (15.15)		140 (84.85)	165 (100.99)	12 (10.62)	11 (9.73)	90 (76.65)	113 (100.00)	37 (13.31)	11 (3.96)	230 (82.73)	278 (100.00)

The trend clearly shows that only very few families are exposed to the education, that too many of them upto primary level. Majority of the parents and siblings are illiterate. The poor literacy level among the parents and siblings of the women clearly indicates that most of the tribal families have no tradition of education and they are negligent of girls education.

(vi) Tradition of Bride Price

Practice of bride price i.e., receiving cash or kind by the brides parents at the time of their daughters marriage from the parcuts of the bridegroom is a common practice in almost all the tribal communities in India. Savara, Cholanaickan and Kattunaickan are no exception to this practice. Bride price in a tribal community indicates many things, it is an economic activity also determines the status of women. The amount of bride price, a woman receives at the time of her marriage depends on her skill in the economic and domestic activities, Better the skills, higher the bride price and higher will be the status of the bride. This tradition indirectly has its impact on the status of women's literacy and education. Even the unmarried tribal girls are more interested in acquiring the skills so that their parents receive more bride price which ultimately represents their higher status.

TABLE 9

Practice of bride price at the time of marriage

S. No.	Item	Savaras	Kattunaickans	Cholanaickans	Total
1.	Received	94 (71.21)	73 (98.65)	0 (0.00)	175 (81.78)
2.	Not - Received	38 (28.79)	1 (1.35)	8 (100.00)	39 (18.22)
	Total	**132 (100.00)**	**74 (100.00)**	**8 (100.00)**	**214 (100.00)**

The table above indicates that 81.78 per cent of the parents of the tribal women have received bride price at the time of their daughters marriage. Only 18.22 per cent have revealed that their parents have not received any bride price at the time of their marriage. But, surprisingly, all the Cholanaickan women reported that their parents did not receive any.

(vii) Work Assignment to the Girl Children

Tribal families as mentioned earlier, train their girls in all economic and domestic activities at an early age. The girl children contribute substantially to the wellbeing in their families. Moreover a tribal girl who is not an expert in domestic and the other economic activities is considered worthless and no man would come forward to marry her. Keeping in view of this fact, an attempt was made to collect the information on the type of work assigned by the parents to their unmarried daughters. The same is presented in the following table.

TABLE 10

Type of work assigned to the women during their childhood

S. No.	Item	Savaras	Kattunaickans	Cholanaickans	Total
1.	Agriculture	32 (24.24)	16 (21.62)	2 (25.00)	50 (23.36)
2.	Forest	87 (65.91)	20 (27.03)	1 (12.50)	108 (50.47)
3.	Domestic work	8 (6.06)	18 (24.32)	5 (62.50)	31 (14.49)
4.	Special occasions like marriage and festivals etc.	3 (2.27)	16 (21.62)	0 (0.00)	19 (8.88)
5.	Others*	2 (1.52)	4 (5.41)	0 (0.00)	6 (2.80)
	Total	**132 (100.00)**	**74 (100.00)**	**8 (100.00)**	**214 (100.00)**

Regularly assigned work is taken into consideration in this context. The information presented in the table indicates that half of them (50.47%) are involved in the work relating to the forest and 23.36 per cent of them are assigned to the agricultural work followed by domestic work (14.49%) and other various roles related ot the occasions like celebration of marriage and other functions (8.89%) etc.

The work assignment in the case of Kattunaickan shows that majority of the women during their childhood were assigned with the forest work (27.02%), domestic work (24.32%) followed by agricultural work (21.62%) and various role during special occasions like marriages and festivals. In the case of Savaras, the women during their childhood were assigned the tasks of forest (65.91%), agriculture (24.24%) and domestic work (6.06%). In some cases, the girls were also given special tasks on the occasions like marriage and festivals.

Even in the case of Cholanaickan, majority of them (62.50%) were involved in domestic work followed by agriculture (25.00%) and collection of minor forest produce (12.50%). The trend of the responses clearly show that girls are involved in various tasks relevant to their later life.

It is reported that the unmarried girls in these tribal communities are capable of undertaking any work assigned to the feminine sex. The type of work assigned to the girls depend on the season. During the agriculture season they attend to agriculture work, if the work is in the forest they attend to it etc. In general unmarried girls among these tribes have no time to think about education.

(viii) Age at which Girls were assigned Work

Majority of the tribal population depends on agriculture and forest resources for their livelihood. It is also true that the tribal parents want to train their girl child in different tasks so as to enable them to lead their lives independently if necessary. As a result, the

the girl children are assigned different types of work at an early age. In view of their involvement in the work at an early age they may not have opportunity to go to the school and are unable to understand the importance of education. Further, their parents themselves are illiterate and are not giving any preference to educate their girl children. The following table provides information about the age at which the girls start their work or assigned work:

TABLE 11

Parental discrimination between daughters and sons

S. No.	Parental Discrimination	Savaras	Kattunaickans	Cholanaickans	Total
1.	Discrimination Exist	53 (40.15)	27 (36.49)	2 (25.00)	82 (38.32)
2	No Discrimination	79 (59.85)	47 (63.51)	6 (75.00)	132 (61.68)
	Total	**132 (100.00)**	**74 (100.00)**	**8 (100.00)**	**214 (100.00)**

59.85 per cent of the Savara tribal women disclosed that their parents did not discriminate between themselves and their male siblings. The remaining 40.15 per cent of them expressed that their parents favoured their male siblings. More or less the similar trend prevails in the case of Cholanaickan and Kattunaickan. As a whole, Savara, Cholanaickan and Kattunaickan women (61.68%) expressed that their parents did not show any discrimination between them and their male siblings. This finding goes against the assumption that the tribal parents discriminate between their sons and daughters.

TABLE 12

Work assignment to Savara children as per their age

S.No.	Age (Years)	Nature of work: Domestic N=132	Forest N=132	Agriculture N=132	Shandy N=132
1.	4-8	65 (49.24)	42 (31.82)	15 (11.36)	0 (0.00)
2.	9-13	38 (28.79)	59 (44.70)	64 (48.48)	20 (15.15)
3.	14-18	29 (21.97)	26 (19.69)	43 (32.58)	46 (34.85)

Half of the sample of the Savara women revealed that they were assigned domestic work at an early age between 4-8 years followed by forest work (31.82%) and agriculture work (11.36%). It is clear that most important work assigned to them is domestic work followed by agriculture and forest work.

(ix) Age at which work assigned to the Girls among Kattunaickans

TABLE 13

Work assigned to Kattunaickan children as per their age

S.No.	Age (Years)	Nature of work: Domestic N=74	Forest N=74	Agriculture N=74	Shandy N=74
1.	4-8	18 (24.32)	8 (10.81)	2 (2.70)	5 (6.76)
2.	9-13	36 (48.65)	21 (28.38)	4 (5.41)	18 (24.32)
3.	14-18	28 (37.84)	25 (33.78)	32 (43.4)	28 (37.84)

Majority of Kattunaickan women (48.65%) revealed that at the age of 9-13 years they are assigned the domestic work, forest (28.38%), agriculture (5.41%), shandy (24.32%) etc.

TABLE - 14

Work assignment to Cholanaickan children as per their age

S.No.	Age (Years)	Nature of work: Domestic N=8	Forest N=8	Agriculture N=8	Shandy N=8
1.	4-8	7 (87.50)	0 (0.00)	0 (0.00)	0 (0.00)
2.	9-13	0 (0.00)	0 (25.00)	0 (0.00)	1 (12.50)
3.	14-18	0 (0.00)	4 (50.00)	2 (25.00)	2 (25.00)

Majority of the Cholanaickan women (87.50%) revealed that they are assigned domestic work at young ages i.e., 4-8 years. After attaining the age of 14-18 years they are given the tasks like collection of forest produce, agriculture and shady work etc.

This indicates that, they have to take part in the household/economic activities of the family at the young age itself making them unaware of educational benefits.

(x) Parental Preference for Daughters and Sons Education

It is assumed that, parents discriminate and give less preference to their girl children in educating them when compared with their male siblings because, they are of the opinion that sons will look after them in their old age and be helpful the them. On the other hand according to them, the girls education is a mere waste in terms of money and resources. It is assumed that, the tribal parents feel that the girls after their marriage shift to their husbands household and the benefits of their education go to their husbands families but not to them.

xi. Tribal Women's Preference for the Sex of the Children

In order to find out the tribal women's preference for boys and girls, the sample women were asked for their choice and the obtained information is presented in the table.

TABLE 15
Tribal women's preference for boys or girls

S. No.	Parental Prefernce	Savaras N = 132	Kattunaickans N=74	Cholanaickans N = 8	Total N=214
1.	Sons	45 (34.09)	7 (9.46)	2 (25.00)	54 (25.23)
2.	Daughters	28 (21.21)	9 (12.16)	0 (0.00)	37 (17.29)
3.	Any one	59 (44.69)	58 (78.38)	6 (75.00)	123 (57.48)

More than half of the women (57.48%) among all the tribes have no particular preference regarding the sex of the children. They liked to have both girls and boys.

Among Savara women 44.69 per cent of them have no particular preference regarding the sex of their children, they liked both girls and boys. On the other hand, 34.09 per cent of the women preferred to have male children, and 21.21 per cent of them preferred to have daughters. Whereas in the case of Kattunaickan most of the women have no particular preference and treated both sons and daughters equally. But, 9.46 per cent of the women preferred to have sons and another 12.16 per cent preferred to have only girl children.

Whereas in the case of Cholanaickan, 25 per cent of women preferred to have sons and rest of them (75.00%) have no particular preference. But, none of the sample women opted for daughters only.

xii. Educational Preferences: Girl or Boys

The preferences of women regarding their sons and daughters education is given in the table below.

TABLE 16

Tribal women preferences for educating their daughters and sons

S. No.	Item	Savaras N = 132	Kattunaickans N=74	Cholanaickans N = 8	Total
1.	Sons only	19 (14.39)	4 (5.41)	0 (0.00)	23 (10.74)
2.	Daughter only	23 (17.42)	6 (8.11)	0 (0.00)	29 (13.55)
3.	Both should be educated	90 (63.18)	64 (86.49)	8 (100.00)	162 (75.70)

The above table clearly indicates that majority of the tribal women expressed that both the sons and daughters should be educated, they gave equal importance to their sons and daughters education. 13.55% of women expressed the need to educate daughters only and 10.74% of women preferred educating their sons only.

Similar trend prevails among Savaras and Kattunaickans. Almost all Cholanaickan women expressed that both sons and daughters should be educated.

(xiii) Attitude towards Girls' Education

To find out the attitude of the tribal women towards education of the girls, the women were asked to reveal their opinion. The results obtained from them are given in the following Table 17:

TABLE 17
Tribal women's attitude towards education of the girls

S. No.	Parental Prefernce	Savaras N = 132	Kattunaickans N=74	Cholanaickans N = 8	Total N=214
1.	Positive	75 (56.81)	9 (12.16)	7 (87.50)	91 (42.52)
2.	Negative	57 (43.18)	65 (87.84)	1 (12.50)	123 (57.47)

The women among the Savara recognized the importance of educating the girls. Nearly 57 per cent of them accepted that their daughters should be educated. But 43 per cent of them did not recognize the need for educating the girls. They stated that there is no use of educating the girls.

Whereas in the case of Kattunaickans, 85 per cent of the women stated that there is no need to educate the girls. Only 15 per cent of them recognized the need for educating the girls.

But, in the case of Cholanaickans majority of the women (87.50%) reacted positively towards educating the girls and only 12.50 per cent of them reacted negatively.

As a whole, more or less similar trend is noticed among Savaras and Cholanaickans.

As a whole, majority of the tribal women reacted against education of girls. On the whole, 42.52 per cent of the sample expressed positive attitude towards educating the girls and rest of them possessed negative attitude. This trend clearly shows their traditional attitude towards women's education.

CHAPTER - V

STATUS OF EDUCATION AMONG THE TRIBAL WOMEN

Despite serious efforts of the Government towards the education of the tribes, the formal system of education has failed in universalising elementary education among the tribes. The reasons attributed are many. The low enrolment of girls in the school, high dropout rate in the first five years of schooling, irrelevant curriculum, non-tribal teachers, difference in language, not used to the system, alien environment, not having immediate benefit, parents apathy, necessity of economic support to the family, indifferent attitude, lack of motivation and aspiration, poor economic conditions, no school within the vicinity, scattered habitations, inconvenient school timings, shortage of teachers participation of children in sowing and harvesting, lack of transport facilities, early marriages, ill equipped schools and hostels, misutilisation of facilities provided to the tribes etc., are some of the factors identified by different research studies responsible for the failure of elementary education among the tribal communities in the country. Keeping in view the above background, an attempt is being made in the following pages to understand the status of education among the tribal women and their opinion towards various aspects of education.

In order to elicit the opinion towards various aspects of education like support of the parents, environment prevailing in the school etc., a number of questions were asked to the selected sample women, Tribal women are grouped into different categories : illiterate married women, literate married women, school going girls and dropouts. The analysis presented in Table 18.

TABLE 18
Distribution of sample according to education and marital status

S. No.	Category	Savaras N = 165	Kattunaickans N=97	Cholanaickans N =16	Total N=278
1.	Married/ Illiterate women	132 (80.00)	74 (76.28)	8 (50.00)	214 (76.98)
2.	Married/ Literate women	33 (20.00)	23 (23.71)	8 (50.00)	64 (23.02)
3.	School going girls	64 (38.79)	16 (16.49)	0 (0.00)	80 (28.78)
4	School dropouts	42 (25.45)	11 (11.34)	0 (0.00)	53 (19.06)

(i) Opinion of the Illiterate Married Women towards Various Aspects of Education

This section presents the information relating to the illiterate married women's reasons as expressed by them for not enrolling themselves in the school during their childhood.

The reasons are arranged in rank order according to their frequency. Findings presented in the above table shows that lack of motivation, personal interest, unawareness about education, domestic work and work in the forest are the most important reasons found to be the main obstacles in pursuing formal education. Early marriage, opposition from the parents, agricultural work, apathy towards girls' education, economic problems and other personal reasons also contributed in keeping away the tribal women in their childhood from the schools. In addition, lack of learning tradition in the family, not giving any thought about education also had their impact.

TABLE 19

Reasons of the illiterate married women for non-enrolment in the school

S. No.	Reasons (Multiple)	N=214	Percntage	Rank
1.	No motivation	66	30.84	1
2.	No personal interest	58	27.10	2
3.	No idea about education at all	46	21.49	3
4.	Pressing domestic work	45	21.03	4
5.	Work in the forest	44	20.56	5
6.	Early marriage	40	18.69	6
7.	Opposition of the parents	39	18.22	7
8.	School is far away from the home	38	17.76	8
9.	Agricultural work	34	17.29	9
10.	Apathy towards girls education	36	16.82	10
11.	Economic difficulties	32	14.95	11
12.	Other personal reasons	30	14.02	12
13.	no tradition of learning in the family	17	7.94	13
14.	Never thought about education	16	7.48	14
15.	Shyness	16	7.48	14
16.	Education not relevant to their life	14	6.54	15
17.	Alien environment in the school	8	3.74	16

a. Reasons Attributed by Savara Married Illiterate Women for not Enrolling in the Schools

An attempt is made to elicit the opinion among the Savara illiterate married women for not enrolling themselves in the school during their childhood (Table 20).

TABLE 20
Reasons of the Illiterate Savara married women for non-enrolment in the school

S No.	Reasons (Multiple)	N=132	Percentage	Rank
1.	No personal interest	41	31.06	1
2.	No motivation	41	31.06	1
3.	Due to heavy domestic work	33.	25.00	2
4.	Work in the forest	30	22.73	3
5.	Agricultural work	25	18.94	4
6.	Early marriage	24	18.18	5
7.	No idea about the education at all	23	17.42	6
8.	Opposition of the parents	21	15.91	7
9.	School is far away	19	14.39	8
10.	Economic difficulties	17	12.88	9
11.	Girls does not require education	16	1212	10
12.	Other personal reasons	16	12.12	10
13.	Never thought about education	12	9.09	11
14.	No tradition in the family	10	7.58	12
15.	Education not relevant to their life	9	6.82	13
16.	Shyness	5	3.79	14
17.	Alien environment in the school	4	3.03	15

The reasons presented in the above table indicates that lack of interest and motivation were found to be the chief reasons for not enrolling themselves in the school followed by domestic work (25.00%), and work in the forest (22.73%). In addition to the above, the other important reasons are agriculture work (18.94%), early marriage (18.18%), no idea about education (17.42%), opposition from the parents (15.81%), location of the school at long distance (14.39%), economic difficulties (12.88%), apathy towards girls education (12.12%) and other personal reasons (12.12%). Further it was also found that there is no tradition of learning in the family, education not relevant to the life, shyness and alien environment in the school were some of the other reasons for not enrolling themselves in the school.

b. Reasons attributed by Kattunaickan Married Illiterate Women for Non-enrolment in the Schools

The responses of the Kattunaickan married illiterate women for enrolment in the school in their early ages reveal that lack of motivation, non-awareness and apathy towards girls education are the main reason Location of the school far away from the home, opposition from the parents, lack of interest had their impact for not attending the school. In addition, early marriages (16.21%), personal reasons (18.91%), agricultural work (16.21%), shyness (14.86%) are some of the other reasons for not attending the schools.

Further, lack of tradition of education in the families, lack of relevance to their life, lack of awareness about the importance of educational alien environment in the school also contributed to the illiteracy of the women.

The responses of Cholanaickan married illiterate women for their non-enrolment into the school are mainly due to early marriages. Half of the sample women felt that due to their early marriage they could not enter the schools. 25 per cent of them revealed that due to the economic difficulties and opposition of the parents prevented them from the school gates. Some of them (12.50%) reported that they have no idea about education, lack of motivation, lack of personal interest, apathy towards girls education, no tradition of learning in the family are the main hindrances for them for their non-enrolment..

TABLE 21

Reasons of the illiterate Kattunaickan married women for non-enrolment in the school

S. No.	Reasons (Multiple)	N=74	Percentage	Rank
1	No motivation	24	30.49	1
2.	No idea about education at all	22	28.05	2
3.	Apathy towards girls education	19	24.39	3
4.	School is far away from the home	19	23.17	3
5.	Opposition of the parents	16	21.95	4
6.	No personal interest	16	20.73	5
7.	Early marriage	14	18.91	5
8.	Economic difficulties	13	18.91	6
9.	Work in the forest	12	17.56	7
10.	Other personal reasons	14	16.21	7
11.	Agricultural work	12	16.21	7
12.	Pressing domestic work	12	16.21	8
13.	Shyness	11	14.86	9
14.	No tradition of learning in the family	6	8.11	10
15.	Education not relevant to their life	5	6.76	11
16.	Alien environment in the school	4	5.41	11
17.	Never thought about education	4	5.41	11

TABLE 22

Reasons of the illiterate Cholanaickan married illiterate women for not attending the school

S.No.	Reasons (Multiple)	N = 8	Percentage	Rank
1.	Early marriage	4	50.00	1
2.	Opposition of the parents	2	25.00	2
3.	Economic difficulties	2	25.00	2
4.	No motivation	1	12.50	3
5.	No idea about education at all	1	12.50	3
6.	Apathy towards girls education	1	12.50	3
7.	No personal interest	1	12.50	3
8.	No tradition of learning in the family	1	12.50	3

c. Location and Non-location of School in the Native Villages

The women are further asked about the location or non-location of the school in their native villages during their childhood and the same information is presented in the table below:

Table 23
Location and non-location of school in their respective villages during the childhood

S.No.	Item	Savara	Kattunaickan	Cholanaickan	Rank
1.	Presence of school	26 (19.70)	8 (10.81)	1 (12.50)	35(16.35)
2.	No School	106 (80.30)	66 (89.19)	7 (87.50)	179(83.64)
	Total	**132 (100.00)**	**74 (100.00)**	**8 (100.00)**	**214 (99.99)**

It is interesting to note that majority of the illiterate married women from the three tirbes expressed that no school was located in their villages during their childhood and before they were married off. Only 19.70 per cent of Savara women and 10.81 per cent of Kattunaickan and 12.50 per cent of Cholanaickan women said that during their childhood schools were located in their villages. The findings clearly indicate that majority (83.64%) of the women from the three tribes did not have access to education within their native villages during their childhood.

TABLE 24
Simple inclination towards going to the school

S. No.	Item	Savaras N=132		Kattunaickan N = 74		Cholanaickans N - 8		Total N = 214	
		Yes	No	Yes	No	Yes	No	yes	No
1.	Inclination towards going to schools	18 (13.64)	114 (86.36)	57 (77.02)	17 (22.97)	4 (50.00)	4 (50.00)	79 (36.92)	135 (63.08)

Responses provided by the women show that about 36.92 per cent of them expressed that they are willing to go to school but could not make it and 63.08 per cent of them never thought of going to the school.

Tribe-wise details shows that majority of Savara women (88.36%) did have any inclination to go to school. On the other hand, majority of the Kattunaickan women (74.39%) are of the opinion that they are willing to attend the schools, but could not make it because of some reason or the other. In the case of Cholanaickan half of them have inclination to go to school whereas the other half did not have any inclination to go to school.

d. Willingness of the Parents for Sending their Children to Schools

After ascertaining the sample women's opinion about their interest in attending the school, further probe was made to ascertain whether their parents are willing to send them to the schools. As per the responses of the sample majority (92.06%) of their parents are not willing to send their daughters to the schools. Similar trend is noticed among all the three tribes.

TABLE 25

Parental willingness for sending their children to schools

S. No.	Item	Savaras N=132		Kattunaickan N = 74		Cholanaickans N - 8		Total N = 214	
		Yes	No	Yes	No	Yes	No	yes	No
1.	Parents opinion for sending their children to schools	6 (4.55)	126 (95.45)	7 (9.46)	67 (90.54)	4 (50.00)	4 (50.00)	17 (7.94)	197 (92.06)

(ii) Opinion of the married literate women towards various aspects of education

This section deals with the opinion of the literate married tribal women towards various issues related to their experience in the school, viz., age of admission into the school, age at which they have dropped out, environment in the school, medium of instruction, opinion towards instruction, work assigned to them in the school, utility of education in their day-to-day life, etc.

Age at which Admission into the School

In order to note the age at which enrolment of the children into the school, the tribal married literate women are asked at what age they are admitted into the achool. The responses of the tribal women are ana!ysed and presented in Table 26.

TABLE 26

Age of the married literate women at the time of school admission

S. No.	Age (Years)	Savaras N = 33	Kattunaickans N = 23	Cholanaickans N = 8	Total N=64
1.	<7	25 (75.76)	16 (69.57)	8 (100.00)	49 (76.56)
2	>7	8 (24.24)	7 (30.43)	0 (0.00)	14 (23.44)

Table 26 shows that 76.56 per cent of the women informed that they are admitted into the schools at the age of 5-6 years and the rest 23.44 per cent are admitted after the age of 7 years. In other words, majority of the literate married women are admitted into the school at their right age. This is an interesting trend which goes against the assumption that in tribal areas of the country children are admitted in to the school at very late age. As per this study, 76.65% of married literate women took admission into the school when they are at the ages between 5-6 years.

b. Age at which discontinuation of schooling

Table presentd below provides the information on the age at which the literate married women discontinued their education.

Table 27
Age at which discontinuation of education

S. No.	Age (Years)	Savaras N = 33	Kattunaickans N = 23	Cholanaickans N = 8	Total N=64
1.	0-5	4 (12.12)	3 (13.04)	2 (25.00)	9 (14.06)
2.	6 -10	5 (15.15)	0 (39.13)	6 (0.00)	11 (42.19)
3.	11 -15	18 (54.55)	9 (39.13)	0 (0.00)	27 (42.19)
4.	16 - 20	6 (18.18)	11 (47.83)	0 (0.00)	17 (26.56)

Table 27 illustrates that 27.27 per cent of Savara women have discontinued their education even before reaching the age of ten years. The trend is similar with 35.48 per cent of Cholanaickan and Kattunaickan married literate women. The drop out rate in the age groups of 11-15 years is high among the Savara and Kattunaickan. But in the case of Cholanaickan all the women dropped out from the schools before they reached the age. On the whole, it is evident from the above table that dropout rate at an early age is high among all the three tribes.

TABLE 28
Educational level at which discontinuation occurred

S. No.	Age (years)	Savaras N = 23	Kattunaickans N = 23	Cholanaickans N = 8	Total N = 64
1.	Primary	29 (87.88)	18 (78.26)	8 (100.00)	55 (85.94)
2.	Upper Primary	4 (12.12)	5 (21.74)	0 (0.00)	9 (14.06)

Table 28 indicates that majority of the tribal women from all tribes, Savara (87.88%) Kattunaickan (78.26%) and Cholanaickan (100%) discontinued their education at the primary level of education itself and a few of them dropped out at upper primary level.

School Environment

The retention and creating interest on education among the children also depends on the environment in which they are placed. Keeping in view of this an attempt is made in this section to elicit the opinion of the tribal women about the school environment when they had education in their early years. The information is presented in the following table:

TABLE 29

Opinion of married literate tribal women towards school environment

S. No.	Item	Savaras N =33		Kattunaickans N=23		Cholanaickans N = 8		Total N =64	
		F	UF	F	UF	F	UF	F	UF
1.	School Environment	7 (21.21)	26 (78.78)	2 (8.69)	21 (9130)	8 (100.00)	0 (0.00)	9 (14.06)	5 (85.94)
2.	Class Environment	6 (18.18)	27 (81.81)	2 (8.69)	21 (91.30)	8 (100.00)	0 (0.00)	8 (12.05)	56 (87.50)

F : Favourable **UF** : Unfavourable

Table 28 shows that 85.94 per cent of tribal women are of the opinion that the environment in the school was not favourable and conducive for them to continue their education. In addition, the classroom environment was also found to be not favourable, probably, this may be the reasons for their dropout from the school.

Surprisingly, though all the Cholanaickan women accepted that they like school and class-room environment, due to some other reasons, they dropped out from the schools.

Medium of Instruction

Savaras, Cholanaickan and Kattunaickan have their own dialect, the regional languages. Telugu and Malayalam respectively are foreign languages to them and have only rudimentary knowledge. The medium of instruction in the schools in both the tribal areas is in the regional languages. The following table provides the information about medium of instruction in the schools where the sample women attended the schools.

TABLE 30
Medium of instruction in the schools

S. No.	Medium	Savaras N = 33	Kattunaickans N = 31	Cholanaickans N = 8	Total N = 64
1.	Telugu	28 (84.85)	---	0 (0.00)	28 (43.75)
2.	Malayalam	---	23 (100.00)	8 100.00)	31 (48.44)
3.	Oriya	5 (15.15)	---	0 (0.00)	5 (7.81)

Table 29 shows that majority of Savara (84.85%) have received education in Telugu language. However, for a few of them who are at border areas medium of instruction was Oriya language. In the case of Kattunaickan and Cholanaickan of they had the education in Malayalam language. All the women of the three tribes expressed that they had difficulties in following the lessons, in the schools because they are not taught in theirr reginal language.

e. Opinion of Tribal Women towards Teaching

A question whether the women were satisfied with the teaching that they had received in the school was asked and the same is presneted in the following Table 31:

TABLE 31

Opinion of the tribal married literate women towards teaching

S. No.	Item	Savaras N=33	Kattunaickans N=33	Cholanaickans N=8	Total N=64
1.	Not Satisfactory	31 (93.94)	23 (100.00)	8 (100.00)	62 (96.87)
2.	Satisfactory	2 (6.06)	0 (0.00)	0 (0.00)	2 (3.13)

It is clear from the above Table 30, that majority of the women (96.87%) from all three tribes were not satisfied with the teaching. It is understandable because the medium of instruction was in regional language in which the women have very little knowledge, under such circumstances no one would be satisfied with the teaching.

f. Work assigned to the Children in the Schools

The type of day to day treatment shown to the students by the school authorities is one of the key factors in motivating, retaining or discouraging the children in the schools. Further, it also has its impact on their scholastic achievement. Treatment by the teachers is looked into in terms of work other than education assigned to the women when they attended the schools.

TABLE 32

Nature of work assignment to the children in the school

S. No.	Name of work	Savaras N=33	Kattunaickans N = 31	Cholanaickans N = 8	Total N = 64
1.	Sweeping	16 (48.48)	15 (65.22)	0 (0.00)	31 (48.44)
2.	Carrying water	2 (6.06)	6 (26.09)	0 (0.00)	8 (12.50)
3.	Not assigned any work	15 (45.45)	2 (8.69)	8 (100.00)	25 (39.06)

It is clear from the Table 31 that majority of the women compained that their teachers used to assign the task of sweeping the premises of the schools, cleaning (48.44%) and fetching of drinking water (12.50%) etc.

The Table 31 also indicates that all the Cholanaickan women reported that they were not assigned any type of work like sweeping, carrying water etc., in the schools. Half of the Savara women also reported that they are not assigned any work, but only 9 per cent of Kattunaickans reported that they were not engaged in any work other than education. As a whole, the above table clearly reveals that majority of them were engaged with the works other than education.

g. Women's Perception about the Utility of Education

An enquiry was made to understand the women's perception about the utility of education in their day to day life. The same is presented in the following table:

TABLE 33

Opinion towards the utility of education in their day-to-day life

S. No.	Item	Savaras N = 33		Kattunaickans N = 23		Cholanaickans N = 8		Total N = 64	
		Yes	No	Yes	No	Yes	No	Yes	No
1.	Usefulness of education	25 (75.76)	8 (24.24)	19 (82.61)	4 (17.39)	8 (100.00)	0 (0.00)	52 (81.25)	12 18.75)

From the above table, it is obvious that 81.25 per cent of the tribal women are of the opinion that the education they have acquired in their younger age is found to be useful in their day-to-day life.

h. Desire of the Tribal Women to Continue their Education

Keeping in view of the goals of the universalisation of education and education for all, the Government of India and respective State Governments have launched a number of schemes for the promotion of education among different categories of people. In this context, women were asked whether they would like to continue their education if given chance and provided facilities. Information provided by the tribal women is presented in the following table:

TABLE 34
Desire of the tribal married literate women towards further education

S. No. Item	Savaras N = 33		Kattunaickans N = 23		Cholanaickans N = 8		Total N = 64	
	Yes	No	Yes	No	Yes	No	Yes	No
1. Desire to continue Their education	13 (39.39)	20 ((60.61)	3 (13.04)	20 (86.96)	8 (100.00)	0 (0.00)	24 (37.50)	409 (62.50)

It appears that majority of the tribal women (Savara and Kattunaickan (62.50%) have not shown any interest to pursue further education, only, 37.50 per cent of them are interested to continue their education, if they were given the opportunity.

It is interesting to note that all the Cholanaickan women are enthusiastic in continuing their education.

(i) Tribal Women's Retention Capacity

In order to identify the extent of literacy retained by the tribal women, the respondents were asked to write their names and read a simple passage. The information is presented in the following table:

TABLE 35
Reading and writing skills of tribal women

S. No.	Name of Work	Savaras N = 33	Kattunaickans N = 23	Cholanaickans N = 8	Total N = 64
1.	Reading	9 (27.27)	2 (8.69)	0 (0.00)	11 (17.18)
2.	Writing their name	24 (72.73)	21 (91.30)	8 (100.00)	53 (82.81)

It is evident from the above table that only 17.18 per cent women can read the scripts. But, 82.81 per cent of them can write their names along with reading ability. Among the three tribes, all the Cholanaickan women reported that they can read and write their names followed by Kattunaickan (91.30%) and Savara (72.73%) women.

(ii) Opinion of the school going girls towards various aspects of education

In order to enhance the literacy rate among primitive tribal groups particularly among women. Government of India established several residential schools and primary schools in their habitations. In the present study and attempt is made to find out how the enrolled girl students are faring in these schools. The information relating to the school and school environment, home work assigned to them, cooperation from their parents and siblings, their further aspirations etc., are collected from the school going girls of the sample households. There are 64 such girls among Savaras and 16 girls among Kattunaickans. There is no representation from Cholanaickans, because the daughters of the sample women are not of school going age.

TABLE 36
Girls studying in the schools

S. No.	Type of School	Savaras (N = 64)	Kattunaickans (N = 16)	Total (N = 80)
1.	Residential	17(26.56)	16(100.00)	33(41.265)
2.	Non-residential	47(73.44)	0(0.00)	47(57.75)

Table 36 shows that among Savara, 26.56 per cent of the girls are in the residential schools and rest are in non-residential schools. Whereas in the case of Kattunaickan all the girl-children are studying in the residential schools. As a whole the above table clearly shows that majority of Savara girls are in non-residential schools while Kattunaickan girls preferred to study in residential schools.

a. Level of Education of Girl-children

The school going girls from the sample households are classified into three groups based on their level of education, such as primary education, secondary education and graduation and the same is presented in Table 37.

TABLE 37
Educational levels of girl-children

S. No.	Level of education	Savaras (N = 64)	Kattunaickans (N = 16)	Total (N = 80)
1.	Primary	46 (71.88)	12 (75.00)	58 (72.50)
2.	Secondary	17 (26.56)	4 (25.00)	21 (26.25)
3.	Gradution	1 (1.56)	---	1 (1.25)

Table 37 indicates that 71.88 per cent of Savara girls are in the primary schools, 26.56 per cent of them are in the secondary schools and very few (1.56%) of them are doing their graduation studies.

More or less similar trend prevails among the Kattunaickan: 75.00 per cent of them are in primary school and the remaining 25.00 per cent are in secondary schools.

b. Medium of Instruction in the Schools

Most of the tribes have their own dialect and those in romote areas have very little knowledge of regional language. But in the schools in tribal areas of the country, medium of instrucation is in regional languages. Table 38 given below gives brief information on the medium of instruction in the schools the girls are studying.

TABLE 38

Medium of instruction taught in the school

S. No.	Medium of instruction	Savaras (N = 64)	Kattunaickan (N = 16)	Total (N = 80)
1.	Telugu	54(84.38)	---	54(67.50)
2.	Malayalam	---	16(100.00)	16(20.00)
3.	Oriya10	10 (15.63)	---	10(12.50)

The above Table 38 shows that for 84.38 per cent of Savara girl students medium of instruction is Telugu and 15.63 per cent of them have Oriya as the medium of instruction. In the case of Kattunaickan for all the respondents medium of instrucion was Malayalam.

c. School Environment

Proper environment in the school would encourage the students to concentrate on their studies and the indirect impact would be less dropouts. Interesting and good environment in the school definitely creates a desire among the students to be regular to the schools.

Environment in this context refers to, aspects like teachers attitude, ability to teach, the availability of teaching and learning material, physical facilities in the school, etc.

TABLE 39
Environment in the school

S. No.	item	Savara (N = 64)		Kattunaickans (N=16)		Total (N = 80)	
		Yes	No	Yes	No	Yes	No
1.	Favourable environment in the school	48 (75.00)	116 (25.00)	12 (75.00)	4 (25.00)	60 (75.00)	20 (25.00)
2.	Level of comprehension of subject	39 (60.94)	25 (39.06)	0 (0.00)	16 (100.00)	39 (48.75)	41 (51.25)

The above table indicates 75.00 per cent of the Savara girl students are satisfied with the existing environment in the schools, only 25 per cent are not satisfied with the school environment. In the case of Kattunaickan, similar trend is observed.

Regarding comprehension of lessons, more than half of the girls among Savaras (60.94%) are able to understand the lessons. In the case of Kattunaickan all the respondents reported that they could not understand the lessons taught in Malayalam, the regional language. Overall 51.25 per cent are not able to understand the lessons taught to them in regional languages.

d. Home Work

Home work will help a student to retain the lessons taught in the classroom. The girl students are further asked about the assignment of home work to them.

TABLE 40
Home Work assigned to the Students

S. No	Item	Savara (N = 64)		Kattunaickans (N=16)		Total (N = 80)	
		Yes	No	Yes	No	Yes	No
1	Home work assigned to the student	59 (92.19)	5 (7.81)	14 (87.50)	2 (12.50)	73 (91.25)	7 (8.75)

It is clear that 91.25 per cent of the girl students reported that they were assigned home work regularly. Looked at from each tribe more or less similar trend is noticed.

e. Other Work assigned in the School

Generally, in rural areas teachers assign some petti works other than education to the students, wasting their time. This is a part of bad environment prevailing in the schools in tribal and rural areas. Assigning other work to the students may ultimately create disinterest in school among the students. Table below shows the position prevailing in the schools attended by the girl students.

TABLE 41
Work assignment other than education

S. No	Item	Savara (N = 64)		Kattunaickans (N=16)		Total (N = 80)	
		Yes	No	Yes	No	Yes	No
1.	Work assignment other than the regular educaiton	45 (70.31)	19 (29.69)	12 (75.00)	4 (25.00)	57 (71.25)	23 (28.75)

Nearly 70.31 per cent of the Savara girl students reported that their teachers assigned work not related to education. Whereas in the case of Kattunaickan, 75 per cent of the girls reported that they were assigned work other than the education. Overall, majority of tribal girl students (71.25%) reported that their teachers assigned them with the work not related to their education.

f. School Curriculum

Curriculum should be relevant to the life of the people. It will help people to enhance their living standards and to retain the attendance in the school. Hence, an attempt is made to ascertain the opinion of the girl students whether the curriculum taught to them is relevant to their life or not. Their opinion is given in the table presented below.

TABLE 42
Curriculum relevant to the life

S. No.	Item	Savaras (N = 64)	Kattunaickans (N = 16)	Total (N = 80)
1.	Curriculum relevant of their life	52(81.25)	16(100.00)	68(85.00)
2.	Curriculum not relevant to their life	12(18.75)	0(0.00)	12(15.00)

Table shows that majority of the Savara girl students (81.25%) and all the Kattunaickan girl students (100.00%) are of the opinion that the present curriculum being taught in the school is relevant to their day-to-day life and only a few of the Savara girls (18.75%) expressed that the curriculum is not relevant to their life. As a whole, 85 per cent of the girl students feel that curriculum being to them is relevant to their day-to-day life.

g Preference for Tribal / Non-tribal Teachers

It is generally assumed that if the teachers working in the schools in tribal areas come from the tribal communities, the tribal students would be better related and adopt themselves to the school. Keeping this in view effort was made to find out the opinion of the girl students on this aspect and the same is given in the following table:

TABLE 43
Preference for tribal or non-tribal teachers

S. No.	Item	Savaras (N = 64)	Kattunaickans (N = 16)	Total (N = 80)
1.	Preference for Tribal Teascher	22(34.38)	1(6.25)	23(28.75)
2.	Preference for Non-tribal teacher	42(65.62)	15(93.75)	57(71.25)

It is seen from the Table that the 65.62% Savara girl students preferred non-tribal teachers and 34.38 per cent of them preferred tribal teachers. In the case of Kattunaickan 93.75 per cent of them opted for non-tribal teachers. Only 6.25 opted for tribal teachers. Overall picture is that 71.25 per cent of the tribal students preferred non-tribal teachers and only 28.75 per cent preferred tribal girl teachers. The assumption that the students in tribal areas prefer tribal teachers to non-tribal teachers seems to be wrong.

h. Home Environment and Education

If the school going children have proper facilities and congenial environment in their homes they would definitely show progress in their education. Following table provides information about the facilities in the home of the girl students.

Table 44 shows that in the case of Savara girls 54.68 per cent of them felt tat their homes have significant light and space to study. In addition, 26.56 per cent revealed that they have suitable environment at home and 4.69 per cent of the girls opined that they have sufficient reading and writing material.

In the case of Kattunaickan 25 per cent of them opined that they have sufficient light and space at home, for reading and 43.75 per cent expressed that they have suitable environment in their homes.

TABLE 44
Suitable facilities at home to study

S. No.	Item	Savaras (N = 64)	Kattunaickans (N = 16)	Total (N = 80)
1.	Sufficient light and space	35 (54.68)	4 (25.00)	39 (48.75)
2.	Suitable environment	17 (26.56)	7 (43.75)	24 (30.00)
3.	Sufficient reading and writing material	3 (4.69)	5 (31.25)	8 (10.00)
4.	No suitable facilities	9 (14.06)	---	9 (11.25)

As a whole, 48.75% of the girl students have sufficient light, only 30 per cent of them are having sufficient space and 10 per cent of them are having sufficient reading and writing materials. It is clear that not all the girl students have satisfactory facilities for home study

i Motivation from the Parents

Encouragement from the parents enhances the interest and creativity among the students to get a good education and how far the girl students received encouragement frcm their parents is the question? The answer is provided in the following table:

TABLE 45
Parental encouragement to the girls to study

S. No.	Item	Savaras (N = 64)		Kattunaickans (N = 16)		Total (N = 80)	
		Yes	No	Yes	No	Yes	No
1.	Motivation from the parents	15 (23.44)	49 (76.56)	0 (0.00)	16 (100.00)	15 (18.75)	65 (81.25)

Table clearly indicates that only 23.44 per cent of the parents of the Savara girl parents encouraged their children in their education, while 76.56 per cent of the parents did not give any encouragement. The students from Kattunaickan were not encouraged by their parents. As a whole, only 18.75 per cent of the sample reported that they are getting their parental encouragement in their education..

j. Aspirations of the Girl Students

Every student will have his / her own aspiration in their lives, a few want to become doctors, a few engineers, etc. The aspirations of the tribal girl students are enquired and the same is presented in the table.

TABLE 46
Aspiration of girls

S. No.	Item	Savaras (N = 64)	Kattunaickans (N = 16)	Total (N = 80)
1.	To get married	26 (40.62)	6 (37.50)	32 (40.00)
2.	To become a teacher	28 (43.75)	8 (50.00)	36 (45.00)
3	To become a doctor	3 (4.69)	1 (6.25)	4 (5.00)
4	To become an engineer	4 (6.25)	1 (6.25)	5 (6.25)
5.	To become a Goverment Officer	3 (4.69)	0 (0.00)	3 (3.75)

It was found from the table, that majority (43.75%) of the Savara and Kattunaickan girl student (50.00%) aspired to become teachers and 40.62 per cent Savara girls and 37.50 per cent of Kattunaickan girls want to get married. On the other hand, 4.69% of them want to become doctors and Government officers respectively and 6.25 per cent of the Savara girls also expressed their ambition to become an engineer. The above trend shows that for majority of the girls from both the groups their role model is their teachers and they want to become teachers.

k. Provision of Reading and Writing Material

Usually the Government will provide books, pencils and pens etc., to the tribal students. Does the girl students receive the reading and writing material? If so where do they get? The table given below provides this information

TABLE 47

Provision of reading and writing material to the girls

S. No.	Item	Savaras (N = 64)	Kattunaickans (N = 16)	Total (N = 80)
1.	Government	43 (67.19)	15 (93.75)	58 (72.50)
2.	Parents	21 (32.81)	1 (6.25)	22 (27.50)

The above table clearly indicates that 67.19 per cent of Savara girls and 93.75 per cent of Kattunaickan girls received reading and writing material from the Government. 32.81 per cent of Savara girls and only 6.25 per cent of Kattunaickan girls reported that they received the same from their parents. As a whole, majority of the girl students received their study material from the Government.

(iv) Opinion of the school dropout: girl children on various aspects of education

42 girls from Savara tribe and 11 girls from Kattunaickan tribe are identified as school dropouts. There is no representation from the Cholanaickan tribe because the daughters of these women are not of school going age. Hence, by interviewing the identified drop-outs and attempt was made to find out the stage at which they dropped out and the causes which made them to drop out from the school.

a. Class from which the Girls Dropped Out

Table 48 provide the information about the class from which the girls dropped out.

More than half of the sample (56.66%) from both the groups discontinued their education at the level of Upper Primary School. Most of the schools are established as residential and are located in mandal headquarters. Hence, the girls have to stay in hostels to continue their education.

TABLE 48
Class from which the girls dropped out

S. No.	Class from which school dropout	Savaras N = 42	Kattunacikans N = 11	Total N = 53
1.	Primary School	5 (11.90)	2 (18.18)	7 (13.21)
2.	Upper Primary School	25 (59.52)	5 (45.45)	30 (56.60)
3.	High School	9 (21.48)	3 (27.27)	12 (22.64)
4.	Intermediate	3 (7.14)	1 (9.99)	4 (7.55)

b. Reasons for Discontinuation of Education

The girls gave several reasons for discontinuing their education, the same are recorded in the Table 49.

TABLE 49
Reasons for discontinuation of education

S. No.	Class from which school droput	Savaras N = 42	Kattunacikans N = 11	Total N = 53
1.	Apathy towards education	3 (7.14)	3 (27.27)	6 (11.32)
2.	Unable to follow the lessons	3 (7.14)	---	3 (5.66)
3.	Stressing domestic work	12 (28.57)	---	12 (22.64
4	Unfavoruable school environment	4 (9.52)	4 (36.36)	4 (7.55)
5.	Ttreatment by the teacher	---	4 (36.36)	4 (7.55)
6.	Interest in outdoor play rather thaen education	6 (14.29)	---	6 (11.32)
7	Marriage at early age	6 (14.29)	3 (27.27)	9 (16.98)
8	Non co-operation of parents	5 (11.90)	1 (9.09)	6 (11.32)
9	Lack of awareness of education	3 (7.14)	---	3 (5.66)

Majority of the Savara girls (28.75%) expressed that stressing domestic work was one of the important reasons for them to discontinue their education. Interest in outdoor play (14.29%), early marriage (14.29%), non co-operation of parents (11.90%), lack of awareness of educational benefits (7.14%) were some of the important reasons for their discontinuation.

In the case of Kattunaickan, teachers' treatment (36.36%) was found to be the major cause discontinuing their education. Getting married at an early age (27.27%), apathy towards education (27.27%), and non cooperation of parents to continue their education were also found to be the reasons.

As a whole, early marriage (16.98%) was found to be the one of the hindrances for discontinuing their education. Apathy towards education (11.32%), stressing domestic work (22.64%) etc., were also some of the important causes for dropping out from the school.

c. Interest in the Continuation of Education

Further, an attempt is made to see how many of them are interested to start their education once again if an opportunity is given and facilities provided. The responses given by them are presented in the following Table 50:

TABLE 50
Interest in continuation of their education

S. No.	Item	Savaras N = 42		Kattunacikans N = 11		Total N = 53	
		Yes	No	Yes	No	Yes	No
1.	Interest in continuation of education	18 (42.86)	24 (57.14)	6 (54.54)	5 (45.45)	24 (45.28)	29 (54.72)

From the above table, it is clear that 42.86 per cent of the Savara girls expressed interest to start their education and again while the rest of the Savara girl students negatived it. Whereas, in the case of Kattunaickan, nearly half of the sample expressed interest in the continuation of education.

d. Preferences for the Type of Schools to Continue their Educa tion

The girls who are interested to restart their education are further asked about the type of school they preferred for continuing their education and two options were given to them, the formal school and the non-formal education.

TABLE 51
Type of school preferred to continue their education further

S. No.	Type of School	Savaras N = 18	Kattunaickans N = 6	Total N = 24
1.	Formal School	13 (72.22)	2 (33.33)	15 (62.50)
2.	Non-formal School	5 (27.73)	4 (66.67)	9 (37.50)

The above table indicates that 62.50 per cent of the girls preferred to continue their education in formal schools rather than in the non-formal system. The trend is similar in the case of both the tribes.

e. Skill in Writing among the Dropouts

To find our whether school drop out girls have retained anything like writing and reading from their school experience they were asked to write their names and the results are presented in the following Table 52.

TABLE 52
Ability to write their own names

S. No.	Item	Savaras N = 42		Kattunacikans N = 11		Total N = 53	
		Yes	No	Yes	No	Yes	No
1.	Ability to write their names	39 (92.86)	3 (7.14)	9 (81.81)	2 (18.18)	48 (90.57)	5 (9.43)

It is evident from table 52, that 92.86 per cent of school dropout girls of Savara are able to write their names. Whereas 81.81 per cent of Kattunaickan are able to write their names properly. With regard to the total sample, 90.57 per cent of girls are able to write their names.

CHAPTER - VI

DEVELOPMENTAL PROGRAMMES OF TRIBES IN ANDHRA PRADESH AND KERALA

Over the Decades Tribal Development Programmes in the country have taken many twists and turns, Immediately after independence, the Government of India thought Development Programmes designed for the general population would also equally benefit the tribal communities. But, unfortunately it did not happen. Next came the establishment of Multipurpose Tribal Development Blocks in the tribal areas covering majority of the tribal population. Again these multipurpose blocks failed to achieve expected results. Finally, the Government of India introduced Integrated Tribal Development Agencies in the tribal areas of the country. The method under ITDA was bringing all the development agencies of the Government under the supervision of ITDA so that sectoral linkages can be taken care of ITDA is responsible today both in planning and execution of all the programmes from land development to education and health in tribal areas. The following pages describe the Development Programmes launched in the tribal areas mainly inhibited by Savara in Andhra Pradesh and Kattunaickan and Cholanaickan in Kerala State.

Developmental Programmes for Tribes in Kerala

Next to Africa, India has the largest concentration of tribal population. Though a lot has been done for their social and economic betterment, yet a great deal remains to be done. Sociologically the concept of development should be looked upon as an organized activity with the aim of satisfying certain basic needs and to psychologically orient the tribals to adopt new skills, attitudes and lifestyles, so that they build up the inner strength and appropriate social and cultural infrastructure to stand the pressures of the new situation and accrue benefits from new programmes and maintain higher levels (Belshan, 1972).

The advent of independence saw a plethora of governmental programmes launched by various official and non-official agencies for the welfare and development of the tribal people. But the first systematic effort for the development of tribal areas was initiated in 1955 in the form of Special Multi Purpose Tribal Development Blocks. A modified version of this programme was taken up on a larger scale during the Second Five Year Plan when the tribal development blocks were started. This programme was further expanded during the Third Five Year Plan and all areas with more that two-third tribal concentration were covered by the end of the period. About 38 per cent of the total tribal population of the country spread over 504 tribal development blocks were covered. Although it was agreed in principle toextend the programme to all the areas which had more than 50 per cent tribal population, it was not possible to do so during the Fourth Five Year Plan.

The programme was reviewed by the Planning Commission and was found that the developmental effort from the general sector programmes was not adequate in these areas, particularly, in the context of their coparatively lower economic base. It was, therefore, decided to evolve a new strategy for the development of the tribal areas.

The pattern of central assistance for plan programmes depends on whether these are centrally-sponsored or state plan schemes. In case of centrally sponsored schemes, states get 100% central assistance and for those in the state plan, central assistance is available as block grants and loans. Classification of centrally-sponsored and state plan schemes are as follows:

a. Centrally Sponsored Schemes

1. Tribal Development Blocks
2. Cooperation
3. Girl's hostels
4. Post-matric Scholarship
5. Coaching and pre-examination training schemes for competitive examination
6. Research, training and special projects.

b. State Plan Schemes

1. Education by providing pre-matric scholarships,.stipends books, stationary, uniforms etc.,
2. Economic development through subsidized agricultural Implements, seeds, fertilizers, animal husbandry etc.,
3. Health, housing and others like drinking water supply,. social and cultural activities etc.

c. Development Profiles of Tribals in Kerala

Majority of the tribals in the state are residing in rural areas with agricultural sector providing them main means of livelihood. Among the total tribals, half of them depend on agriculture but only 17 per cent are the cultivators and the remaining are distributed in various other occupations including agriculture labour.

The tribes have the monopoly in the collection of minor forest produce. Food gathering, hunting and fishing are the subsistence activities.

As a part of total literacy programme of the State, a sub-project, for tribal literacy programmes was lauched in September 1991 to make nearly 64,000 tribals literate but the programme could not achieve the desired level of impact in certain remote tribal pockets, Hence, to bridge the gap and to consolidate the literacy status already achieved by the tribes, the State Saksharatha Samithi launched the post-literacy and C.E among these communities. These programmes covered not only literacy, but included several other items incidental to the culturall and socio-economic advancement of the tribes.

Integrated Tribal Development Agency was launched to initiate intensive developmental programmes in the tribal areas.

Developmental Programmes

1. Education

In all the Five Year Plans, priority was given to educational development of Scheduled Tribes. The main reason for the very slow spread of education among Scheduled Tribes is the isolated nature of their habitations. Majority of them are living in remote areas far away form institutions. The social and economic conditions prevailing in the tribal settlements are not conducive to the spread of literacy, isolation, poverty, exploitation, suppression etc., curtailed effective educational development among STs. Moreover, the parents of the tribal children being generally illiterate neither attach much importance to education nor the children attend classes regularly. In order to promote education among the tribal people, the primary effort should be on the eradication of poverty. The parents of the tribal children should be provided with regular employment for earning income to meet their day-to-day requirements which would probably motivate them to send their children to the school.

The ITDA project has opened Creches / Balawadis / Nursery Schools in tribal areas which will not only promote early childhood education, but also decrease the burden of elder children in looking after their younger siblings. For the promotion of education among the tribes, the ITDA instituted scholarships, provided free hostel facilities, incentives to the parents, free books, pens and pencils, free uniforms, stationary and stipends.

2. Health and Nutrition

Since, the tribal settlements are situated far away from hospital and health centres, the tribal people are not able to make use of medical facilities. Endemic ailments like malaria is found in all the tribal areas. The ITDA authorities started mobile medical dispensaries both Ayurveda and Allopathy and Midwifery Centered at Gram Panchayats. The health department conducted medical camps every year in the tribal areas. Patients with serious diseases were referred to Taluk/District hospitals and financial assistance is provided for their treatment. Provision is also made in annual plan for extending financial assistance to voluntary organizations engaged in health related services in the tribal areas. As recommended by the Monitoring and Steering Committee on SC/ST. Development of formulation of IX Plan, suitable rules and regulations for ensuring the presence of doctors and paramedical staff are to be framed at the earliest.

3. Housing

The problem of housing among tribals is very crucial. During the IX plan high priority is given for tribal housing. For the proper execution and monitoring of housing programmes uniform rates for the various agencies engaged with tribal housing have been introduced. Housing is one of the schemes transferred to Block Panchayats.

Apart from the above measures, the ITDA took up following measures to protect the tribal rights.

4. Bonded Labour

The identified bonded labourers will be rehabilitated and they will be provided with regular employment, housing and other basic amenities.

5. Land Alienation

Alienation of land is a serious problem in the tribal areas of India. Several causes are responsible for large scale land alienation in tribal areas. Tribal people largely depend on non-tribals to meet their credit requirements even though it may eventually result in disposal of their land in some way or the other. The socio-economic survey .of tribals conducted by the Economics and Statistics Department during 1976-78, reveals that tribals alienate their lands mainly for meeting their domestic expenses including socio-religious ceremonies and medical treatment.

Of late many tribes have started approaching the state sponsored cooperative credit societies for credit but still the cooperative credit but still the cooperative credit societies in tribal areas are under utilised. Another factor for their approaching the local money lender is that the cooperative societies advance onlyshort-term loans for productive purposes while most of the tribals need loans for consumption and subsistence purposes and cooperative societies are unable to meet them.

Taking into consideration, the three bases of land alienation of tribal people viz., (a) the lacunae in the laws, (b) the ignorance of the tribal people and (c) the complicated legal procedures to be followed, various State Governments have been doing something to help the tribals. Under them the Government of Andhra Pradesh enacted an Act called A.P. Scheduled Areas Land Transfer Regulation, 1959 and Kerala Government passed the Act viz., "Kerala Scheduled Tribes (Restriction Lands) Act, 1999. As per these Acts, transfer of tribal lands to non-tribals in invalid. But if the area of land transferred to the non-tribal is less than 2 hectares, such transaction are valid . In such cases, the affected tribal is entitled to get an equal extent of land from Government. The Act also mentions that all the landless tribals in the state would be given a minimum of 1 acre of land. Moreover, all the tribals in the state who possess less than 1 acre of land is eligible for getting the remaining part from the Government so as to make the minimum land possessed by them at least is one acre.

6. Minor Forest Produce Collection

From times immemorial, tribal have been living in the forests, collection of forest produce and hunting are two traditional means of livelihood for them. Consequently on the nationalization of Forests, hunting was banned in the country. The right to collect Minor Forest Produce from forests was exclusively assigned to the SC/ST. Cooperative Development Federation from 1978. As per the guidelines issued by the Ministry of Social Justice and Empowerment, Government of India, at least 75 per cent of the sale value of MFPSA, should reach the collecting tribals.

The Forest Department exempted tribal cooperatives engaged in MFP collection from paying royalty or least rent. This is advantageous to both societies and tribals. The Government of India has also approved an Action Plan costing Rs. 356 lakh prepared by the SC/ST Cooperative Development Federation for improving collection, storage and marketing of MFPs. The Federation has utilized the amount released by the Government of India for meeting the margin money requirement and for the construction of godowns.

7. Forest Policy

The Forest Conservation Act, 1980 prevents several development activities in the tribal areas. Apart form the TSP of Forest Department, they are using generated funds under World Food Programme for launching various family oriented / infrastructure based programmes. For solving the problem of tribals living in forests, the Forest Department has prepared a comprehensive perspective plan.

8. Excise Policy

Because of the peculiar and isolated nature of the tribal habitations of the tribal population, no separate excise policy seems to be possible. However, so as to release the tribals from the habit of drinking manufacture and sole of liquors is prohibited in the tribal areas.

i. Atrocities

Large scale atrocities against tribals are seen in the country. In order to prevent the atrocities against them, Prevention of Atrocities Act, 1989 was implemented. For a speedy disposal of cases registered under the Atrocities Act, a special bench is instituted in all district courts.

ii. Developmental Programmes of Tribes in Andhra Pradesh

(a) Profile of the Study Area

The agency area of the Vizianagaram District covers an area of 22 sq.km. with a tribal population of 1,53,344 which works out to 8.5% of the district population. The tribal population is mainly spread over 455 village in the mandals of Karupam, Salur, Parvatipuram, Pachipenta, Makkuva, Komarada and G.L.Puram.

As per 1991 Census, the total number of households are 3,83,292; among them SC houlseholds are 35,943 and ST housholds are 37,158; the total population covered is 22,05,057 with SC population is 1,79,783 whereas the ST population is 1,85,729.

The ITDA in Vizianagaram District started functioning with its headquarters Vizianagaram from 3rd march, 1980. Subsequently, in the year 1982 the head quarters of ITDA is shifted to Parvathipuram keeping in view, the proximity to the tribal sup-plan area. The main objective of the ITDA is to identify the problem of tribals inhabiting the contiguous groups of villages called the sup-plan tribal area, signifying the area based approach to the problems with a view to formulate viable and firm strategies in an integrated manner to achieve socio-economic development of the tribals and also to improve infrastructure and standard of administration in the tribal area. The project area called Tribal Sub-Plan also includes all the 298 scheduled villages and another 151 non-scheduled villages where there is a sizeable tribal population. Thus, the sub-plan area is spread over 449 villages in 8 mandals of the district. There are also 36 villages which become contiguous in 5 mandals which are called cluster villages.

Parvathipuram agency area has 8 sub-plan mandals and covers 595 inhabited village and 28 un-inhabited villages; ST household in the sub-plan area are 3000; ST men population of the sub-plan mandal is 75,901; ST women population in sub-plan mandal is 76,484; the total population of sub-plan villages came to about 1,79,400 and whereas the tribal population is 1,42,693. Among the total men tribal population is 71295 and women number 71,398. Thus, the percentage of tribal population is 78.95. Tribe wise population: Jatapu - 44,090; Kondadora - 38,161 and Mookadora - 1,101; Gadaba population is 31,178 while the Savara population it covers 29,162.

The total literates are 1,24,887 (27.6%). The total men literate population is 82,804 (36.17%) and women literates are about 42,083 (18.51%)

The cattle in tribal areas are of poor quality, it applies both to milch cattle and drought animals. In fact very few tribals keep milch cattle because they are not used to consuming milk and milk products. On the other hand, the tribals keep brought cattle for agricultural purposes. Keeping goats and pigs is generally found in these communities. Stall feeding of cattle is very rare and the cattle depend on grazing in the forest areas.

The veterinary institutions are catering to the needs of the livestock in the tribal areas. One mobile ambulatory clinic with head quarters at Bhadragiri is functioning. The veterinary team goes around the villages in a van provided by the DRDA.

During the year 2000-01, 3,76,528 cases were treated, 22,234 castrations were made, 6,41,232 were vaccinated in the scheduled areas to control contagious and non-contagious diseases among the livestock by the Annual Husbandry Department staff.

b. Developmental activities of ITDA, Parvathipuram, Vizianagaram District since inception i.e., from 1980-81 to 2001-02

The ITDA Parvathipuram is reaching out to the poorest of the poor living in remotest parts on hill top villages which were not covered so far. The ITDA has covered 13,313 beneficiaries under agriculture scheme; 59,380 beneficiaries are under horticulture; 5491 beneficiaries are under minor irrigation; 794 SHGs are found in the agency area. The total number of beneficiaries are 94,412 under different schemes with a total budge allocation of 2302.24 lakhs.

1. Education

The ITDA has opened residential, non-residential schools and libraries for children, 92 school buildings were opened with financial grant of 77.48 lakhs; 140 Anganwadi buildings with financial grant of 146.36 lakhs; 65 Quarters, 36 Ashram schools, 14 boys hostels, 6 girls hostels, 2 Residential ITI, 1 Ashram school complex, 36 guest houses, libraries IFAD. All the above buildings have been constructed at a cost of 1381.93 lakhs. Total 478 students are being educated in these schools. Action is initiated on the teachers who are irregular in their duties.

2. Agriculture

Under agriculture development programme, 445 acres are covered with a total grant of 3.930 lakhs. The grant is spent on paddy demonstration and groundnut demonstration plots.

3. Electricity

So far 46 villages in this area have been electrified. Majority of the tribal villages in this area have yet to be electrified.

4. Medical and Health

Under jurisdiction of Parvathipuram agency area, total 11 Primary Health Centres, 2 Government hospitals, 2 Subsidiary Primary health Centres and 4 Mobile Centres are working.

5. DWCRA and Self-Help Groups

433 SHGs, 794 Mahila mandals; 361 DWCRA Groups are found in this area and have received a matching grant of 54.60 lakhs.

CHAPTER - VII

SUMMARY

Most of the tribal communities in India are geopraphically isolated, economically, socially backward and politically weak, but culturally rich and behaviourally simple and trustworthy, leading their life in the lap of nature. They are facing a multiplicity of problems and difficulties forcing them to lead a life at subsistence level and in a few cases full of poverty, deprivation, disadvantages and even varied kinds of miseries and sorrows, very difficult to be effectively tackled by their own effort. Due to lack of education, the tribals lagged behind in acquiring new skill required for their sustainable upliftment. Recognizing that literacy is the instant solution for bringing out immediate change in the life styles of the tribals, high priority was accorded to literacy programmes.

When one looks at the literacy rates among the tribes in India, except in a few cases the rate of literacy is below the general population. It is much more among the tribal women. There are many factors which hinder progress of education among the tribal communities in general and among tribal women in particular. One needs to go deep into the tribal life to understand the factors which inhibit educational progress among the tribes as well as to find out the factors which promote progress of literacy. The present study makes and attempt to find out the factors inhibiting as well as promoting literacy among the tribal women of Andhra Pradesh and Kerala States.

The sample women are categorized into four groups, viz., married literate women, married-illiterate women, school dropouts and school going girls. This exercise is carried out against the background of socio-cultural practices of the tribes. For this purpose, Savara of Andhra Pradesh, Kattunaickan and Cholanaickan of Kerala State have been selected. All the three tribes put together a total of 278 families have been selected as sample.

The profile of the heads of the tribal families selected for the study shows that nearly one-third of the families are headed by the men in all the tribes. Majority of the women heading the families are widows or divorced. Majority of the heads of families come from the age group of 21-40 years i.e., younger age groups. The heads of the families, except among Cholanaickan among whom all the heads of the families are engaged in collection of minor forest produce are mainly engaged in cultivation. This clearly indicates their high degree of backwardness. Literacy point of view, majority of the heads of the families are illiterate and rest of the household heads are literate upto primary level. Similar trend prevails even in the case of women headed families.

All the women selected from the families for interview are married. Majority of the women were married when they were between the age of 11-15 years. The educational background of the sample families shows that very few families are exposed to education and even here only upto primary education. In other words, most of the parents and siblings of the women are illiterate. It is also found that majority of the parents have received bride price. With regard to the occupation, majority of the sample women before their marriage were involved in day-to-day work like agriculture, and forest related activities. They were initiated into the work at the age of 14 and above. There is discrimination between boys and girls in terms of preference and education. Most of the sample have felt that there is no need to educate their girls.

i. Married Literate Women

In the case of married literate women, most of them are enrolled in the schools at the age of 5-6 years. However, majority of them discontinued their education even before reaching the age of 10 years i.e., discontinued their education at primary level itself. It appears that the environment prevailing in the school and classroom seems to be not favourable and conducive for them to continue their education. Further, majority of the sample of all categories complained that they had difficulties in following the lessons in schools because they were not taught in their dialect but in the state languages. As a result, majority of them are not satisfied with the instruction. Added, to this, the children are assigned the work of sweeping and carrying water in the school, etc. Thus, the students are engaged with work other than education. Majority of the women are of the opinion that education is useful in their day-to-day life and it was reflected in their skills of reading and writing, however, they do not want to continue their education further.

ii. Married Illiterate Women

Majority of the married illiterate women have expressed that they could not enroll themselves in the schools due to various reasons such as lack of interest, motivation, not having the idea of education at all, apathy towards education, pressing domestic work and forest related activites, early marriages, parents opposition, etc. In addition, most of the women in native villages do not have schools and the parents are also not willing to send their daughters to schools. Majority of the women in all the three groups of tribes do not have any inclination to go to schoo!. Majority (92.06%) of the sample parents are not willing to send their daughters to schools.

iii. School going Girl Children

It appears that half of the school going girls are day scholars, studying in primary schools. The medium of instruction is in regional languages of Telugu and Malayalam. The school environment is conducive to their learning; 91.25 per cent of girls reported that they are assigned home work regularly and 71.25 per cent of the girls reported that their teachers also assigned work not related to their education. They have also given an understanding that the curriculum is relevant to their environment. Surprisingly, more than half of the girls preferred non-tribal teachers rather than tribal teachers. Very few of the girls are getting parental encouragement in their education. Majority of them aspire to become teachers. One-third of the girls have received support from their parents in procuring the reading material and the rest of them are depended on the Government.

iv. School Dropout Girl Children

School dropout rate seems to be very high among the girls studying in 6th and 7th standards. The reasons for their discontinuation are mainly apathy towards education, stressing domestic work interest in outdoor play, non-cooperation of parents, early marriages, etc. Half of the sample expressed their desire to pursue their education further if given the opportunity through the formal school system. Among the dropout girls, 90.57 per cent of the girls have retained their basic skills of reading and writing.

CHAPTER - VIII

STRATEGIES FOR THE PROMOTION OF LITERACY AMONG TRIBAL WOMEN

In view of the findings presented, the following strategies are suggested for improving the rate of literacy among tribal women:

- The existing formal school system should be strengthened by opening additional residential schools exclusively for girls education. Primary schools should be started in all the tribal habitations irrespective of the size of the habitations;

- The school/classroom environment should be improved and girls should feel homely; they should be provided with all facilities like school uniforms, free reading-writing materials, etc. School/classrooms and surroundings should be kept neat and clean.

- Work unrelated to education should not be entrusted to the students. If other work is assigned to the students; their self-esteem is undermined and it in turn may cause dropping out from the school. Along with formal schooling, they should also be provided with the need based vocational training facility;

- The teachers recruited in tribal schools should be bilingual; they should know the regional language as well as the dialect of the tribes among whom the school is located;

- The dropout rate among children especially girls are more due to poverty, apathy, early marriage etc. Hence, programmes should be organized to create awareness among the parents, stressing the immediate need for educating their daughters;

- Adult Literacy Centres should be opened in all the tribal hamlets without adhering to the norm of minimum size of the centres and by providing all minimum facilities required such teaching learning materials, lighting, equipment, etc.;

- All the developmental programmes that are undertaken in the tribal areas should be incorporated in the learning process so that the students will have proper awareness of these development programmes. Further, this may act as one of the motivating factors to attend the Adult Education Centres:

- The services of the teachers, functionaries of Adult Literacy and Development Programmes of the tribal areas should be recognized and special amenities and incentives may be provided so as as to motivate and attract good teachers to the tribal areas;

- Tribal parents should be persuaded not to perform their daughters marriages at an early age. Further, they should be discouraged not to be take bride price;

- To leave sufficient free time to their children to pursue their education, the tribal parents should be convinced and persuaded not to entrust work in the house as well as outside the house.

- The tribal parents should be persuaded not to discriminate between their sons and daughters not only with regard to their ededucation but also in all the othe raspects of their lives.

APPENDIX - I

A SCHEDULE TO STUDY THE FACTORS AFFECTING LITERACY AMONG TRIBAL WOMEN

FAMILY PARTICULARS

1 Village :

2. Mandal :

3. District :

4. Name of the Tribe :

5 1 .Name of the head of the family :

2. Details of the Members :

Sl. No	Name	Relation -ship to the head	Age	Sex	Marital	Occupa- tion	Education Level	Education Presently in the School	Education Drop
1.									
2.									
3.									
4.									
5.									
6.									
7.									

6. Information about uneducted married women :

6.1 Name :

6.2 Birth Place :

6.3 Age at Marriage :

6.4 Level of education of the parents and siblings :

Relation	Education	
	Level	Dropout
Father		
Mother		
Brothers:		
1.		
2.		
Sisters:		
1.		
2.		

6.5 Whether there is a school in her native village : Yes/No

6.6 If 'yes' upto what standard :

6.7 If 'no' mention the location of the school nearest to her birth place :

6.8 Did you ever thought of going to school :

6.9 Did your parents ever thought of sending you to school :

6.10 If 'No' give reasons :

6.11 If 'Yes' why did not they send you to school :

6.12 Why you did not attend the school to get educated :

S. No	Reasons	Check with ✓ mark
1.	Girls does not require education	( )
2.	Early marriage	( )
3.	No personal interest	( )
4.	No motivation	( )
5.	Opposition of the parents	( )
6.	No tradition in the family	( )
7.	School is far away	( )
8.	Due to heavy domestic work	( )
9.	Work in the forest	( )
10.	Agriculture work	( )
11.	Economic difficulties	( )
12.	Shyness	( )
13.	Alien environment in the school	( )
14.	Education not relevant to their life	( )
15.	Never thought about education	( )
16	No idea about education at all	( )
17.	Any other reasons	( )

6.13 Did your parents receive the bride price at the time of marriage :

6.14 If' 'Yes' why bride price ?

6.15 Before marriage what was your daily routine at your parents house :

(from morning to bed time)

6.16 Type of work assigned to to you before marriage (mention the type of work in each category) :

1. Agriculture
2. Forest
3. Domestic
4. Social occasions like marriage and festivals etc.
5. Any other

6.17. Did your parents show any discrimination in attitude between the daughters and sons : Yes /No

If 'Yes' what type of discrimination

6.18 At what age you began to work in the (mention the type of work in each category) :

S. No.	Loacation	Age	Nature of Work
1.	House (Domestic)		
2.	Forest		
3.	Agricultural fields		
4.	Shandy		

6.19 Do you prefer to have sons or daughers Sons ( ) Daugher ( ) Both ( )

6.20 If 'Sons' alone why ? :

6.21 If 'Daughters' alone why ?:

6.22 If both why ?

6.23 Do you think that both sons and daughers should receive education : Only sons ( )
Only daughter ( )
Both ( )

6.24 If only sons, why not daughters :

6.25 What are the advantages and disadvantages ofeducating the girls :

B. Particulars about married women who discontinued her/their studies :

1. Name :

2. Place of Birth :

3. Age at Marriage :

4. Name of the School studied :

5. Age at which admitted :

6. Age at which education was discontinued :

7. At what level education : Discontinuation took place

8. Why did you discontinue : (a)

(b)

(c)

(d)

(e)

(f)

9.	Describe the environment in the school and class	:	Did you school ( ) yes Class ( ) Yes/No
10.	Did you like it	:	Yes/No
11.	Medium of instruction	:	
12.	Did you understand the teaching	:	Yes/No.
13.	What is the attitude of teachers towards you and other girl students	:	
14.	Were you assigned any work in the school	:	1. Sweeping 2. Carrying water 3. Cleaning etc. 4. Any other work
15.	What was the attitude of boy student towards you and other girl students	:	
16	Can you read and write now if 'Yes' ask her to put her signature below	:	Yes / No 16.1

16.1

17. Was your education useful to you in your day-to-day life : Yes/No

17.1 If 'Yes' what way :

17.2 If 'No' why not :

18. Are you interested to pursue your education now : Yes/No

19. What is your opinion about educating your daughters :

C. Information about the girls presently in the school : Residential Non-Residential

1. Name :

2. Name of the School :

3. Class Studying :

4. Medium of Instruction :

5. Do you like the school and the school environment

6. If 'Yes' what are the aspects you like

6.1. If 'No' why? :

7. Are you able to understand the lessons : Yes/No

8. If 'No' why? :

9. Tell us about your daily :

	routine in the school		
10.	Do the teachers give homework daily	:	
11	What is the attitude of teachers towards you and other girl students	:	
12.	Do they assign you any work other than education	:	Yes/No
13.	If 'Yes' what type of work	:	
14	What is the attitude of the boy students towards girl students	:	
15.	What do you think about the curriculum in the school	:	1. Relevant to the life ( ) 2. Irrelevant to the life ( )
16.	Whom do you like to teach you	:	Tribal Teacher/non-Tribal Teacher
17.	What work is assigned to you in the house everyday	:	
18.	Do you attend the school in time	:	Yes/No
19.	Do you frequently absent yourself from the school	:	Yes/No
20.	Would you like to continue your education	:	Yes/No
21.	If 'Yes' upto what level ?	:	

21.1.	If 'No' why?	:	
21.2	Conveniences available at house to do home work and to read	:	Sufficient light Sufficient space Sufficient reading and writing material
21.3	At what time you do your home work	:	
22.	Does your parents encourage you in your studies		Yes/No
22.1	If 'No' why ?	:	
22.2	If 'Yes' what way	:	
23.	Do you have proper clothing to put on when you go to school	:	Yes/No
23.1	How many pairs of clothing you have		
24.	Do you have all the materials like text books, note books, pen, pencil, etc	:	Yes/No
24.1	If 'Yes'who gave you those materials	:	
24.2	If 'No'did not you buy them	:	
25.	What do you eat before yougo to school daily	:	
26.	Do you think your male	:	Yes / No

siblings are well treated by your parents when compared to you and to your sister

26.1 If ' Yes' why ? :

27. After completing education what are your aspirations
1. To get married
2. To become a teacher
3. To become a doctor
4. To become a engineer
5. Govt. officer
6. Any other

D. Information about recent dropouts (within the past five years) :

1. Name :

2. School Attended :

3. Class from which dropped out

4. Year of dropped out :

5. What are you doing at present

6. Why did you dropout (Please check the reasons) : Reasons
1. No interest
2. Difficult to follow the lessons
3. Work in the house
4. Did not like the environment
5. Did not like the teachers
6. Teacher's attitude was not good

7. Students attitude was not good
8. Interested in outdoor play
9. Got married
10. Opposition of the parents
11. School was located in another village
12. No use of education
13. Any other

7.	If given chance are you interested in continuing your education	:	Yes/No
7.1	If Yes, would you like to go to regular school or adult education centre	:	
7.2	If 'No' why ?	:	
7.3	Can you write your name	:	Yes/No
7.4	If 'Yes' write your name below	:	

BIBLIOGRAPHY

Ambassht, N.K.(1970), *A Critical Study of Tribal Education,* New Delhi, S. Chand & Co.

Bhatnagar, R. (1985), *The Expectations of Girls Studying at Non-formal Education Centres*, SIERT, Rajasthan.

Bose, A.B. (1970), "Problems of Educational Development of Scheduled Tribes," *Man in India*, Vol. 50.

Das Gupta, N.K. (1964), *Problems in Tribal Education and the Santals,* Bharatiya Adimajathi Sevek Sangh, New Delhi.

Dave, V.G. (1981), *A Survey of the Position of the Implementation of Non-formal Education in Rajasthan,* SIERT: Rajasthan.

Dhebar, U.N.(1962), *Report of the Commission for Scheduled Area and Scheduled Tribes,* Ministry of Home Affairs, New Delhi, Vol. 1 : 224-227.

Elwin, Verrier (1960), *Report of the Committee on Special Multipurpose Tribal Blocks,* Ministry of Home Affairs, New Delhi.

Galbraith, John Kenneth (N.A), *Economic Development in Prespetive*, United States Information Service, New Delhi.

Gupta, Daljit (1983), *A Critical Study of Non-formal Education Programmes (age group 9-14) Run by Different Agencies in the State of Madhya Pradesh,* Ph.D.Thesis in Education, Bhopal University, Bhopal.

Joshi, N.D. (1999), *Socio-Cultural and Educational Conditions of Adivasis in Kerala,* Ph.D.Thesis in Education, Kerala University.

Joshi, T.S. (1999), *Acceleration of Tribals in Transition* edited by Tripathuy, Discovery Publishing House, New Delhi.

Kantha, Rishi, Dutta, Narain (1984), *Evaluating the Effectiveness of Adult and Non-formal Education Schemes in Haryana State* SCERT, Haryana.

Karunakaran, K. (1980), *Identification of Factors to be Tackled in an Effective Programme and Training of Farmers,* Ph.D.Thesis, University of Kerala, Trivandrum.

Kumar, R.Y., *School System and Tribal Community: A Study on Scheduled Tribes of Bhadragiri Block,* Ph.D. Thesis, Andhra University.

Mahapatra, L.K.(1953), *Ashram Schools Boarding Schools'* Paper 2nd Conference for Tribes and Tribal Areas, Bharatiya Adimajathi Sevak Sangh, Delhi, pp. 148-54.

Mohapatra, R. (1988), *A Socio-economic Analysis of Inter-district Educational Disparity at School Level in Orissa,* Ph.D. Thesis, Utkal University, Orissa.

Mullick, S.P. (1981), *Development of Learning Materials for Non-formal Education of Girls in the Age Group 11-14 years in Rural Areas,* Dept. of Teaching Aids, NCERT.

Murthy, S.K. (1986), *Evaluation Study of Non-formal Education at Elementary Stage in Andhra Pradesh from Adminstration Point of View,* Directorate of School Education, Andhra Pradesh.

Nadeem Hasnain (1990), *Tribal India Today,* Harnam Publications, New Delhi.

Nani Panthulu, J. (1986), *An Evaluation of Academic Aspects of Non-formal Education of 9-14 Aged Group,* Directorate of School Education, Andhra University.

Patel, L.K. (1989), *A Study of the Problems of First Generation Learners in Standards I to IV in Ahmedabad City,* A.G. Teachers College, Ahmedabad.

Pillai, K.S. (1991), "Idetification of Motivation Facilitating Factors as well as Barriers in the Adult Education Programme with Reference to Scheduled Castes and Scheduled Tribes Women in Kerala" *CAEE Research Bulletin,* University of Kerala, pp. 79-81.

Pratap, D.R. (1971), *Study of Ashram School in Tribal Areas of Andhra Pradesh,* TCRTI, Hyderabad.

Rahman, M.S. (1978), *Development of Population Education Curriculum in a System of Non-formal Education for Out-of-School Youth,* Ph.D. Thesis, Delhi University.

Rajya Lakshmi, K. (1986), *An Evaluative Study of Certain Aspects of Non-formal Education Programme for Children Aged 9-14 Years in Rayalaseema Area,* Ph.D. Thesis, S.V. University.

Ramana, G.V. (1989), *Problems of Education Among the Tribal Communities of Andhra Pradesh: A Case Study of Ashram Schools,* Ph.D. Thesis, S.V. University.

Sachchidananda (1964), "Tribal Education in India", *Vanyajathi,* Vol. 12(1), pp. 3-6.

Sachchidananda (1967), *Socio-economic Aspects of Tribal Education,* Report of the National Seminar on Tribal Educationl in India, NCERT, New Delhi, 99-108.

Sajith Babu, G.P. (1990), *Barriers in the Implementation of Adult*

Education Programmes Among SCs and STs in Kodakkal a y a t, M.A. Dissertation, Kerala University.

Shah, A.J. (1979), *A Critical Study of the Programmes of Non-formal Education in Baroda City and their Impact on the community*, Ph.D. in Education, M.S. University of Baroda.

Sivarajan, N.K. (1983), *Facilities and Constraints in Providing Non-formal Education for Harijans*, Ph.D.Thesis, Calicut University,

Srivastava, L.R.N. (1964), *Some Basic Problems of Tribal Education, Report on the National Seminar on Tribal Education in India*, N.C.E.R.T.

Srivastava, L.R.N. & Gupta, B.S., *A Study of Methods, Processes and Practices of Non-formal Education Programme for Tribal Students*, NCERT.

Sujatha, K. (1980), *An Investigation into the Constraints on Education of the Nellore District Yanadis with a view to suggest Some Strategies of Non-formal Education*, Ph.D. Thesis, Andhra University.

Talesara, Hemlata (1988), *Tribals and Education: A Quest for Integration in the Regional Mainstream*, G.S. Teachers College, Udaipur.

Tripathy, S.N. (1999), *Tribals in Transition*, Discovery Publishing House, New Delhi.

Vengaiah, S. (2001), *Continuing Education Needs of the Tribal Women in Chittoor District*, M.Phil. Thesis, S.V.University